The Ultimate Evil

The Fight to Ban Nuclear Weapons

Douglas Roche, O.C.

With a Foreword by Judge Mohammed Bedjaoui,
Former President of the International Court of Justice

For Dr. Janine Brodie with Respect Roch Deglas November 6/97

James Lorimer & Company, Publishers
Toronto, 1997

James Lorimer & Company Ltd. acknowledges the support of the Department of Canadian Heritage and the Ontario Arts Council in the development of writing and publishing in Canada. We acknowledge the support of the Canada Council for the Arts for our publishing program.

Questions or comments may be e-mailed to the author at: djroche@gpu.srv.ualberta.ca The author's home page is located at: www.ualberta.ca/~djroche

Cover design: Kevin O'Reilly; cover illustration: Geoff Butler

Canadian Cataloguing in Publication Data
Roche, Douglas, 1929—
          The ultimate evil
ISBN 1-55028-590-4 (bound) ISBN 1-55028-589-0 (pbk.)
1. Nuclear disarmament.   I. Title.
JX1974.73.R62 1997   327.1'747   C97-931878-5

James Lorimer & Company Ltd., Publishers
Egerton Ryerson Memorial Building
35 Britain Street
Toronto, Ontario
M5A 1R7

Printed and bound in Canada

Contents

For my granddaughter, Isabelle Eva Roche Hurley,
and all the grandchildren in the world.

Foreword: Fear and Madness in a Dance of Death

On the threshold of the Third Millennium, humanity has the capability to destroy all life and civilization on the planet several times over through the use of a mere fraction of the nuclear weapons in the world's arsenals. A product of the stirring, and at the same time terrifying, adventure of mankind's scientific and technological advance, nuclear weaponry has surreptitiously become a part of the human condition. Shall we then have to resign ourselves to it? Definitely not! Such is the powerful message of this book.

Written in the wake of the indefinite extension of the Non-Proliferation Treaty, the adoption of the Comprehensive Test Ban Treaty, and two Advisory Opinions delivered by the International Court of Justice *The Ultimate Evil: The Fight to Ban Nuclear Weapons* is a strong but realistic plea in favour of complete nuclear disarmament.

Here, Ambassador Douglas Roche explores, in great detail, the moral and legal arguments against nuclear weapons. Based on widespread and thorough discussions between the author and a great number of representatives of Canadian civil society, this book effectively reflects the concerns of world public opinion, a less and less silent majority.

More than half a century ago, the Atlantic Charter promised people "freedom from fear" and the San Francisco Charter promised to "save succeeding generations" from the scourge of war. There is still a long way to go. Relations among states have always been influenced by the military forces available, but the relationship between nuclear forces and diplomatic action cannot be measured by reference to the usual objective criteria. None of the nuclear powers is responsive to the popular common-sense view that "superiority" and "inferiority" are meaningless beyond a certain destructive capacity. They are continuing to stockpile instruments of death beyond any possible "need." This is indeed "overkill" let loose. In this regard, Ambassador Roche dryly reminds us that "one thermonuclear bomb can have an explosive power greater than that of all the explosives used in wars since the invention of gunpowder."

The nuclear powers assert the doctrine of deterrence, the *raison d'être* of which is to discourage an aggressor from the use of nuclear weapons that could inevitably turn out to be damaging to itself as well. The doctrine of deterrence and "balance of terror" is, in fact, based upon the postulate that one should avoid, by every possible means, occasioning any kind of nuclear confrontation. The advocates of this doctrine point out that it is able to guarantee, not only the national security of a state, but also international stability, by its ability to bring to nought any inclination to take an initiative with nuclear weapons. One should nevertheless not lose sight of the negative consequences of deterrence, which have occasioned an interminable race to develop and accumulate ever-more-sophisticated nuclear weapons. As Ambassador Roche puts it: "In the event of a nuclear exchange, the strategy of nuclear deterrence leads to mutual assured destruction: thus the famous acronym MAD."

In the present stage of scientific development, nuclear weapons can be expected to cause indiscriminate death and unnecessary suffering among combatants and non-combatants alike. The very nature of this blind weapon therefore has a destabilizing effect on humanitarian law, which regulates discernment of the type of weapon used. Although the principle of respect for non-combatants and civilians has been proclaimed as the primary rule of humanitarian law, civilians have been the main victims of major conflicts. The Promethean emergence of nuclear weapons among the means of destruction openly flouted the universal rule of protection of the civilian population.

Humanitarian law continues to prohibit the use of weapons with indiscriminate effects liable to cause unnecessary suffering, and it therefore cannot be regarded as authorizing the use of nuclear weapons, which are incapable of avoiding such effects. By analogy, the interpretation of a number of humanitarian conventions implies a ban on nuclear weapons. For example, exposure to radiation is analogous to exposure to poisonous, harmful, or deadly substances prohibited since the nineteenth century by the Hague Regulations of 1899 and 1907. And even if interpretation by analogy were ruled out, to say that the use of nuclear weapons was legal would give rise to an absurd and untenable situation for international law, because it would mean that the 1925 Geneva Protocol prohibiting the use of asphyxiating gases could not be extended to include the far more lethal clouds released by nuclear explosion.

The prohibition of nuclear weapons, virtually an imperative of humanitarian law and a condition for its very existence, cannot, however, be achieved by treaty law within the framework of the negotiation of international law. It must be achieved within the context of disarmament.

The 186 states that are party to the Non-Proliferation Treaty have undertaken to pursue and conclude negotiations on general and complete disarmament. This treaty can therefore be considered as "central to the ability of the world community to develop peacefully as we journey into the Third Millennium." The obligation to pursue and to conclude negotiations is enshrined in Article VI of the Treaty, but this provision merely crystallizes, or indeed codifies, an undoubtedly customary obligation, the constituents of which began to form in the very first months of the existence of the United Nations. This obligation, contained in repeated and unanimous resolutions of the United Nations General Assembly, in fact applies to the whole of the international community. The International Court of Justice recognized that there is an obligation not only to *pursue* but also to *conclude* negotiations in good faith. This recognition is, definitely, in the very words of Ambassador Roche, "the highest-level legal push ever given to governments to get on with nuclear disarmament."

In this connection, I must underline that the World Court has probably never subjected the most complex elements of a problem to such close scrutiny as it did when considering the problem of nuclear weapons, as witnessed by the unusual duration of the deliberations — almost eight months — which, after the ones that led to the judgement in the South West Africa case in 1966, are the longest in the history of the Court. In its 1996 Advisory Opinion on the legality of the threat or use of nuclear weapons, the Court underlined that:

> In the long run, international law, and with it the stability of the international order which it is intended to govern, are bound to suffer from the continuing difference of views with regard to the legal status of weapons as deadly as nuclear weapons. It is consequently important to put an end to this state of affairs; the long-promised complete nuclear disarmament appears to be the most appropriate means of achieving that result.

I have obviously no desire either to approve or to gainsay the views expressed in Chapter IV of this book relating to the Court's Advisory Opinion. However, I would like to stress that, as mentioned on pages 48-49, I was one of the seven judges who voted in favour of sub-paragraph E of paragraph 2 of the operative part of the Opinion, but my vote must be interpreted in light of my declaration, in which I explained the use of my casting vote as President. Indeed, I emphasized "the fact that the Court's inability to go beyond this statement of the situation can in no manner be interpreted to mean that it is leaving the door ajar to recognition of the legality of the threat or use of nuclear weapons." In the same spirit, I also underlined that "the use of nuclear weapons by a State in circumstances in which its survival is at stake risks in its turn endangering the survival of all mankind, precisely because of the inextricable link between terror and escalation in the use of such weapons. It would thus be quite foolhardy to set the survival of a State above all other considerations, in particular the survival of mankind itself." The meaning of my vote is therefore clear.

Ambassador Roche rightfully draws our attention to the dramatic consequences of non-implementation of Article VI of the Non-Proliferation Treaty, which can jeopardize the whole Treaty itself. He points to the danger of proliferation, reminding us that if errors can occur even in the reliable systems of the nuclear powers there is a high potential for mistakes in the systems of new states acquiring nuclear weapons. In the same vein, Ambassador Roche mentions seven countries that are considered to be of prime proliferation concern today, namely India, Iraq, Iran, Israel, Libya, North Korea, and Pakistan. The reasons for such risks of proliferation must obviously be searched for in the geo-politics of the regions concerned. It is eventually a regional application of the doctrine of deterrence and "balance of terror." The problem of "high-risk" countries is part of the more general problem of regional security, and should be addressed accordingly.

The medical world teaches us that madness is not a contagious disease. But international policy obeys different rules. The proliferation of nuclear firepower is by no means under control, despite the existence of the Non-Proliferation Treaty. So fear and madness may still link arms to engage in a final dance of death. Peoples are still subject to perverse and permanent nuclear blackmail. A way has to be found of delivering them from it. Conceived by Ambassador Roche as "a wake-up call to energize the public to demand that governments ... conclude negotiations on the complete elimination of nuclear weapons," this book will, I believe, play its part in this work of salvation for humanity.

Judge Mohammed Bedjaoui
Former President of the International Court of Justice

Introduction:
A New Sense of Urgency

Over the past quarter of a century, in my work as a parliamentarian, diplomat, and educator, I have come to the conclusion that the abolition of nuclear weapons is *the* indispensable condition for peace in the twenty-first century. Nuclear weapons are the greatest threat to human civilization and to humanity's survival. During the Cold War, the elimination of nuclear weapons was considered impossible, but with its end, a window of opportunity has opened. This opportunity must be seized before the window closes.

Today, many people think that the nuclear weapons issue has evaporated. They are wrong: the present situation is perilous. The five acknowledged nuclear states — the United States, Russia, Britain, France, and China — are determined to maintain their immense stocks of nuclear weapons well into the next century. This is bound to lead to the proliferation of nuclear weapons in other countries: in fact, India, Pakistan, and Israel already possess nuclear weapons although they have not acknowledged as much. Proliferation will eventually lead to use, either through accident, terrorism, or political decision. The use of nuclear weapons anywhere would be a human catastrophe and could potentially repeat itself to unimaginable proportions. A continuation of the present trend, in which the most powerful countries rank their outmoded nuclear doctrine above the development of international law, poses the gravest consequences for humanity.

The most flawed of all the Cold War assumptions carried into the new age is the belief that the strategy of nuclear deterrence is essential to a nation's security. Maintaining nuclear deterrence into the twenty-first century will impede, not aid, the cause of peace. Nuclear deterrence prevents genuine nuclear disarmament and maintains an unacceptable hegemony over non-nuclear development for the poorest half of the world's population. It is a fundamental obstacle to achieving global security.

Those who say that the elimination of all nuclear weapons is impossible forget that at previous periods in history, slavery, colonialism, and apartheid all appeared unalterable. Now they are gone, because the conscience of humanity demanded it. This book, then, is a wake-up call intended to energize the public to demand that governments adhere to the unanimous call of the International Court of Justice (the World Court), the highest legal authority in the world, to conclude negotiations on the complete elimination of nuclear weapons. But how can negotiations be concluded when they haven't even started?

This book is informed but not technical, realistic but not fatalistic, hopeful but not starry-eyed. Most of all, it is human-centred. In my years as a Member of Parliament and as Canada's Ambassador for Disarmament, I have been in far too many diplomatic and political discussions where the human dimension was lost in professional jargon. Here, I want to concentrate on the pre-eminent fact that nuclear weapons contravene humanitarian law, which has been accepted through the centuries as the only fundamental basis for civilization's survival.

Here, the legal and moral arguments against nuclear weapons intertwine with the strategic: since nuclear weapons can destroy all life on the planet, they imperil all humanity has ever stood for, and humanity itself. This is why the President of the World Court, Mohammed Bedjaoui of Algeria, called nuclear weapons "the ultimate evil." In fact, he adds, the existence of nuclear weapons challenges "the very existence of humanitarian law." During the acrimonious years of the Cold War, with its emphasis on the military doctrine of nuclear deterrence as a constant justification for the nuclear arms race, the public felt powerless to stop the relentless build-up of nuclear firepower. But now, in a post-Cold War era characterized by East-West partnership, there is no excuse for continuing to abide the assault on life itself that nuclear weapons represent.

This book emerged out of a remarkable set of roundtable discussions in eighteen cities in all ten provinces of Canada throughout September 1996, sponsored by Project Ploughshares, an ecumenical peace and justice organization. Attending were a total of 404 people in a range of occupations including Members of Parliament, members of provincial legislatures, mayors, city councillors, bishops, clerics, university professors, teachers, physicians, lawyers, judges, journalists, editors, First Nations leaders, directors of foundations, labour leaders, peace activists, school board trustees and administrators, and students.

By engaging a wide range of community leaders and activists, including people and constituencies not usually associated with disarmament advocacy, the roundtables were intended to make the point that all levels of community (from the international to the local) have an opportunity, and a responsibility, to face the reality of the nuclear threat and to demand concrete action.

I was asked to serve as a resource person and discussion leader. A booklet setting out the case for the abolition of nuclear weapons was prepared for the participants. A twenty-two-minute video, *Eliminating Nuclear Weapons,* produced by the Center for Defense Information in Washington, was shown at the beginning of each meeting. Every gathering included someone whose job it was to produce a report. All eighteen of these were synthesized into a national report, which was presented to the federal government. It recommended that Ottawa review its nuclear-weapons policies. The government accepted this recommendation, and asked the Parliamentary Committee on Foreign Affairs and International Trade to begin the review. The American government, along with the United Kingdom and France, protested that Canada was even reviewing its nuclear weapons policies.

There was a sense of amazement, widely expressed at the roundtables, of how little the general public seems to know about important events over the past year — events which have restored the issue of nuclear weapons to a central place on the international agenda. The public is not clamouring for Ottawa to foster and promote a comprehensive program for the elimination of nuclear weapons. On the other hand, public sentiment certainly does not support the retention of nuclear weapons. But when the situation was laid out at the roundtables — the World Court has called for the *conclusion* of nuclear disarmament negotiations and the untenability of ongoing possession of nuclear weapons by the five nuclear states while the rest of the world is proscribed from obtaining them — a sense of urgency for action emerged among the participants. This led to discussions of future education programs and efforts to get the media to pay more attention to an issue central to the post-Cold War global security agenda. It was noted that the Internet is a communications revolution that bypasses the mainstream media with its instantaneous sharing of information. It gives people the potential of being better informed today than ever before. But getting information on the Internet requires a motivation to seek it out. The public is certainly not yet at that stage, and so public opinion, still largely formed by the mainstream media, continues to be largely unaware of the vital work of war prevention. Many roundtable participants said the lack of active public opinion should not be used by government as an excuse not to take a strong stand on implementing the World Court's opinion that the abolition of nuclear weapons is essential.

Many participants remarked that the abolition issue speaks directly to Canadian values. We pride ourselves on being a peaceful people, though when the circumstances of this century demanded, we fought for our liberty. But with the rise of the United Nations, international law, and institutions and mechanisms dedicated to building conditions for peace, recourse to war in order to resolve disputes has lost any attractiveness it ever had for Canadians. Left to itself, it is unlikely that Canada today would join any military alliance or support the maintenance of nuclear weapons. Ottawa's support for the expansion of NATO stems from Alliance pressure, not from popular demand at home. Our national consciousness is alert to promoting peace through the United Nations, not to preparing for war.

It was noted at the roundtables that the ambiguity in Canada's position on nuclear weapons reflects, in some ways, the ambiguity in Canadians themselves. For example, while professing to scorn violence we have become inured to it — on the streets, in our institutions, in our entertainment. It is little wonder that we give so little thought to the violence we share in being part of a system that threatens to use nuclear weapons, thus killing countless individuals who have every bit as much a right to life as we do. Several participants thought it unlikely that we can root nuclear weapons out of our military system until we root violence out of our society.

These discussions led to a general recognition of nuclear weapons as the pinnacle of a system of violence that increasingly has economic overtones as well as military ones, and a further recognition that the subjects of nuclear weapons and violence constitute the supreme moral issue of the day. Many participants, and not only clergymen, called upon our churches, temples, and mosques to do much more to sensitize Canadians to the effects of the toleration of violence. In this respect, the need for community-based organizations to speak out against violence — violence at home and abroad, violence brought about through economic as well as military means — was emphasized.

The roundtables demonstrated that Canadian values are firmly rooted in the pursuit of peace. Significant cross-sections of Canadian society would welcome and rally behind a clear commitment by Ottawa to work immediately — not in the distant future — to secure a program that will lead to the abolition of nuclear weapons.

PART ONE

The Greatest Threat
to Humanity's Survival

1

An Assault on Humanity

When I visited Mayor Takashi Hiraoka of Hiroshima and Mayor Icco Itoh of Nagasaki during a trip to Japan in the spring of 1997, I asked each of them for a message to the Canadian Parliamentary Committee on Foreign Affairs and International Trade, which was then beginning a review of Canada's policies on nuclear weapons. Mayor Hiraoka wrote the Committee: "We, the citizens of Hiroshima, who have suffered a nuclear bombing, deeply believe that the development and possession of nuclear weapons is a crime against humanity, and that nuclear weapons and humankind cannot coexist." Mayor Itoh replied: "Based on our experience, the people of Nagasaki have been appealing to the world that nuclear weapons are lethal, that they could annihilate the human race, and that genuine world peace cannot be attained as long as nuclear weapons exist on this planet."

I tabled these letters when I testified before the Committee as part of a Project Ploughshares presentation. We asked the Committee to examine the moral and strategic arguments against nuclear weapons: their uselessness, the risk of disastrous war they pose through accident, miscalculation, madness, desperation, or terrorism, the immorality of participation in potential mass murder, the repercussions of the continuing disparity among the nuclear haves and have-nots.

The logic of the case for the elimination of nuclear weapons is overpowering, but logic by itself moves neither governments nor the public. In fact, my own views are more strongly rooted in the human dimensions of the Hiroshima and Nagasaki tragedies than they are in logic. I was sixteen when the first atomic bombs were dropped on Hiroshima and Nagasaki in early August 1945. It was only years later, on my first visit to Japan in the mid-1970s, that the horror and scale of the destruction made a lasting impression on me. As the years go by, memories of World War II dim, and I notice that my students deal with the destructive capacity of nuclear weapons in an even more superficial and abstract way.

If the modern movement to abolish nuclear weapons is to make an imprint on the general public, the unimaginable horror of nuclear weapons must be faced. Mayors Hiraoka and Itoh have done a service to this movement by bringing the full story of nuclear devastation to the World Court. In 1994, the World Court was asked to decide on the legality of nuclear weapons. The Mayors' testimonies were given as evidence in the case. Here are the stories they told.

At 8:15 on that fateful morning of August 6, 1945, as World War II was drawing to a close in the Pacific, the American atomic bomb exploded 580 metres above the heart of Hiroshima. It contained a small amount of uranium-235 and produced the energy equivalent of 15,000 tons (15 kilotons) of TNT. An intense flash of light flooded the city centre. With the roar that followed, enormous pillars of flame burst toward the skies, as most buildings crumbled and many people died or were injured. Old and young, male and female, soldier and civilian — the killing was utterly indiscriminate. The entire city was exposed to the compound and devastating effects of thermal rays, shock-wave blast, and radiation.

The Hiroshima bomb generated intense heat that shot out from a fireball about 280 metres wide. The thermal rays emanating from it instantly charred any human being outdoors near the hypocentre (the surface point directly below the explosion). As far as two kilometres from the hypocentre, people's clothing burst into flames. Fires ignited simultaneously across the city, reducing it to char and ashes.

After the initial shock wave, an extremely powerful wind of nearly 1,000 miles per hour tore through the city. People were lifted and carried through the air by this blast. All wooden buildings within a radius of about two kilometres collapsed: many well beyond that distance were badly damaged. The blast and thermal rays combined to totally burn or collapse 70 percent of the 76,327 dwellings in Hiroshima at the time.

There was also radiation damage. Immediately after the explosion, the area was bathed in high levels of initial radiation — gamma rays and neutrons. Within a radius of about one kilometre of the hypocentre, nearly everyone who suffered full body exposure to radiation died. Those who initially managed to survive soon succumbed to the radiation's after-effects. Many not directly exposed to the bomb approached the hypocentre to offer help and sickened or died due to residual radiation. Even today, thousands of people struggle daily with the curse of radiation illness.

On August 6, there were approximately 350,000 people in Hiroshima. Some 140,000 of them were dead by the end of December, 1945. Entire families were wiped out, and the local community was in disarray. Records were lost to fire, and so even today we have no truly accurate casualty figures. Among the dead were Koreans, Chinese, students from throughout Asia, and even a few American prisoners of war.

Hospitals were in ruins, medical staff were dead or injured, and there were no medicines or equipment. Despite their own burns and injuries, survivors worked frantically to help others, but after a few days or weeks, fever, diarrhoea, hemorrhaging, and extreme fatigue claimed many more lives. This was the pattern of the acute symptoms of A-bomb disease. Along with burns and external injuries, initial radiation brought disease and other maladies. Those exposed near the hypocentre suffered widespread destruction of cells and loss of blood, resulting in tissue and organ damage. Immune systems were weakened and symptoms like hair loss were conspicuous.

These acute effects subsided after about four months, but five to six years after the bombing a dramatic increase in leukemia and other later effects were recorded. Keloids (excessive growth of scar tissue over healed burns), cataracts, and various cancers added to the death toll. Those exposed in their mothers' wombs were often born with microcephalia, a syndrome involving mental retardation and incomplete growth.

Sadako Sasaki was exposed to the bomb at the age of two. She appeared to grow up strong and healthy, but ten years later, in 1955, she was suddenly diagnosed with leukemia and hospitalized. Cranes are a symbol of longevity in Japan, and Sadako believed she would be healed if she folded 1,000 paper cranes, so, every day, lying in bed and using the paper her medicine came in, she folded cranes. Despite her hopes and efforts, she died after eight months of fighting.

The story of Sadako's death and her paper cranes touched the hearts of children all over the world. They collected money and built a monument in Hiroshima's Peace Memorial Park. The statue, set high on a pedestal, depicts a young girl holding a giant paper crane over her head. Now, people from Japan and throughout the world continually send their offerings of paper cranes to be placed at the foot of the monument. Through the death of a young girl from the late effects of radiation, paper cranes have become a nearly universal symbol of world peace and the abolition of nuclear weapons.

Mayor Itoh's testimony to the World Court told of how, three days after the Hiroshima attack, an American bomber abandoned its primary target of Kokura because of poor visibility and flew to its secondary target, Nagasaki. That city was also covered by clouds, but the plane was running short of fuel, so when the bombardier caught a glimpse of the city through a crack in the clouds, he hastily released the second atomic bomb.

The Urakami district of Nagasaki was home to a large Christian population that had kept the light of faith alive during a long period of persecution from the seventeenth through the nineteenth centuries. The bomb laid the neighbourhood to waste and instantly killed 8,500 of the 12,000 Christians living there. It was later discovered that the original target for the bombing had not been the Urakami district, which lies in the northern part of Nagasaki, but rather the very centre of the city. If the bomb had exploded over the densely populated city centre, Nagasaki likely would have been obliterated.

The Mayor of Nagasaki at the time recorded the effect of the explosion:

> The explosion of the atomic bomb generated an enormous fireball, 200 metres in radius, almost as though a small sun had appeared in the sky. The next instant, a ferocious blast and wave of heat assailed the ground with a thunderous roar. The surface temperature of the fireball was about 7,000°C, and the heat rays that reached the ground were over 3,000°C. The explosion instantly killed or injured people within a two-kilometre radius of the hypocentre, leaving innumerable corpses charred like clumps of charcoal and scattered in the ruins near the hypocentre. In some cases not even a trace of the person's remains could be found. A wind of over [680 miles per hour] slapped down trees and demolished most buildings. Even iron-reinforced concrete structures were so badly damaged that they seemed to have been smashed by a giant hammer. The fierce flash of heat meanwhile melted glass and left metal objects contorted like strands of taffy, and the subsequent fires burned the ruins of the city to ashes. Nagasaki became a city of death where not even the sounds of insects could be heard.

After a while, countless men, women and children began to gather for a drink of water at the banks of nearby Urakami River, their hair and clothing scorched and their burnt skin hanging off in sheets like rags. Begging for help, they died one after another in the water or in heaps on the banks. Then radiation began to take its toll, killing people like a scourge [of] death expanding in concentric circles from the hypocentre. Four months after the atomic bombing, 74,000 people were dead and 75,000 had suffered injuries, that is, two-thirds of the city population had fallen victim to this calamity that came upon Nagasaki like a preview of the Apocalypse.

There is a poem in the Nagasaki Atomic Bomb Museum written by a ten-year-old girl that tells how her younger sister was trapped under the ruins of their house, how fires were breaking out among the debris, and how their mother — who had suffered severe burns in the bombing — squeezed out her last ounce of strength to save the younger child. The author's mother died before the end of the day, her two-year old sister died thirteen days later, and her five-year old brother died after about two months. No trace remained of her grandmother or her aunt's seven-member family. Her father died of cancer thirteen years ago, and now the author herself is also sick in bed.

A photograph in the Nagasaki museum shows the carbonized corpse of a boy perhaps four years old who was exposed to the bombing near the hypocentre. When she saw this photograph, Mother Teresa, the late Nobel Peace Prize laureate, said, "All the leaders of the nuclear states should come to Nagasaki to see this photograph."

A fourteen-year old boy exposed to the Nagasaki bombing two kilometres from its hypocentre described his experience as follows:

The air-raid shelter in Sakamoto-machi was filled with the dead and injured. The area near the shelter was strewn with corpses, some scorched black and others half-naked with puffed-up faces and skin hanging off like rags. It filled me with sorrow to see, among these, the corpses of a mother clinging to her newborn baby and her three other children lying dead nearby. I could do nothing for the people screaming for help from under the ruins of houses or the people crawling along the ground dragging their burnt skin and begging for water. These screams of agony in the throes of death echoed in the ruins all night. When my father found a pot in the ruins and used it to draw water from a stream, the injured drank it greedily but then lay down and died on the ground. The following morning the screams had subsided, leaving only a world of death like a hell on Earth.

This boy's four-year-old sister died August 10, and his mother, who had suffered severe burns, died August 17. Then, twelve years later, his father died of stomach cancer.

The most fundamental difference between nuclear and conventional weapons is that the former release radioactive rays at the time of explosion. Everyone exposed to large doses of radiation generated during the first minute after the Nagasaki explosion died within two weeks. Not only people directly exposed, but also those who came into the area of the hypocentre after the bombing and those exposed to fallout carried by the wind, suffered radiation-induced injuries. A high incidence of disease was observed among survivors exposed to large doses of radiation. Leukemia, malignant tumours, and other maladies appeared after long periods of latency. The descendants of survivors will have to be monitored for several generations to clarify the genetic impact, and so generations to come will be forced to live in anxiety.

Nagasaki Mayor Itoh concluded his description of the atomic bomb's effects on his city by telling the World Court:

> With their colossal power and capacity for slaughter and destruction, nuclear weapons make no distinction between combatants and non-combatants or between military installations and civilian communities; moreover, the radiation released by these weapons cannot be confined to specific military targets. It can only be said, therefore, that nuclear weapons are inhuman tools for mass slaughter and destruction.

The Development of Nuclear Deterrence

The suffering caused by the bombing of Hiroshima and Nagasaki was immense. However, those original atomic bombs were primitive by today's standards. Their explosive power was about 15 kilotons, 15,000 tons of TNT. In subsequent years, vastly more powerful nuclear weapons were developed as new technologies emerged to make weapons and their delivery systems ever more efficient and deadly. Bombs in the megaton (equivalent to a million tons of TNT) and multiple-megaton range, even up to twenty megatons, were developed. A one-megaton bomb carries almost 70 times the explosive power of the Hiroshima and Nagasaki bombs. A five-megaton weapon would represent more explosive power than all the bombs used in World War II. Huge arsenals of awesome destructive power were amassed during the Cold War in a seemingly never-ending search for security based on the threat of mass devastation.

At the peak of the Cold War, there were more than 70,000 nuclear warheads in existence, and the point had long been passed where all the nuclear weapons in the world had the destructive power to destroy all life on the planet many times over. The fact that there have been post-Cold War reductions in numbers does not lessen the assault on humanity nuclear weapons represent, for the use of even a few of them could wreak intolerable damage on the life-support systems of the planet.

The doctrine of nuclear deterrence became the basic military strategy of both Washington and Moscow during the Cold War. Under nuclear deterrence, both sides profess to have enough firepower to launch a successful retaliatory strike after taking the first nuclear blow of the opponent. The aggressor's destruction is thus assured, the elemental fact that keeps the aggressor from striking in the first place. In the event of a nuclear exchange, the strategy of nuclear deterrence leads to mutual assured destruction: thus the famous acronym MAD.

The theory of nuclear deterrence was first used by the West to prevent a Soviet invasion of Western Europe. Growing numbers of post-Cold War analysts now cast doubt on the assumption that the Soviet Union ever had the intention, let alone the capability, of such an invasion. Nonetheless, throughout the Cold War the Soviets were portrayed in the Western media as an enemy deserving nuclear incineration. The dogma of deterrence encouraged exaggerated, moralistic rhetoric directed at domestic constituencies as well as foreign opponents. This increased international tensions by fueling the arms race and fostering a paranoid approach to arms-control negotiations. Threatening greater evil than it sought to prevent, the deterrence strategy echoed the communist line that the end justifies the means. As nuclear arsenals grew, the explicit threat to the Soviet Union evolved into an implicit threat to the planet. Nuclear deterrence made it "moral" to put the world at risk.

Nuclear weapons differ from conventional ones in three important respects. First, the amount of energy released by an atomic bomb is a thousand or more times greater than that produced by the most powerful TNT bombs. Secondly, a nuclear explosion is accompanied by highly penetrating and harmful radiation, as well as intense heat and light. Thirdly, the substances that remain after an explosion are radioactive and continue to harm living organisms for many years.

Nuclear weapons represent a qualitatively new step in the development of warfare. One thermonuclear bomb can have an explosive power greater than that of all the explosives used in wars since the invention of gunpower. In addition to the immensely magnified destructive effects of blast and heat, they introduce a new agent — ionizing radiation — which extends lethal effects over both space and time.

The Effects of Nuclear Radiation

Ionizing radiation causes cell damage that may destroy the cell or diminish its capacity to function. The meltdown of the Chernobyl nuclear reactor provided an opportunity for the study of the effects of radiation. Thyroid cancers, many diagnosed in children, are 285 times more prevalent than before the accident. Radiation damage is not just local, but extends to the neighbouring territories of Belarus and Sweden. Apart from long-term effects such as keloids and cancers, Chernobyl victims suffered short-term anorexia, diarrhoea, cessation of production of new blood cells, hemorrhage, bone marrow damage, damage to the central nervous system, convulsions, vascular damage, and cardiovascular collapses.

The effects of nuclear radiation are not only agonizing, they are also spread out over a lifetime. Death after a long life of suffering still occurs in Hiroshima and Nagasaki, more than half a century after atomic bombs hit those cities. Birth deformities following radiation exposure are yet another tragedy. In Japan, many deformed children were born to the victims of Hiroshima and Nagasaki: they and their children have defective genes that transmit deformities to succeeding generations. There are also numerous examples of "jellyfish" infants born in the Marshall Islands, a site of atmospheric nuclear testing in the early days of the Cold War. These babies are born with no bones and transparent skin.

The danger to the present environment is so great, a United Nations' study on the environmental effects of a nuclear war coined the phrase "nuclear winter." It showed that fires caused by large-scale nuclear bombings would inject huge quantities of light-absorbing smoke particles into the atmosphere. Sunlight, which warms the Earth's surface and provides the energy that drives the atmospheric processes and biological production, would be reduced by the smoke and soot, altering the weather and influencing the global climate. Among the adverse effects would be cooling of up to 25-30°C over the land mass of the northern hemisphere and the rapid transfer of smoke to the southern hemisphere. The darkness, cooling, and radiological effects would disrupt life's patterns.

The socio-economic consequences of nuclear war in a world intimately inter-connected economically, socially, and environmentally would be grave. Patterns of production, distribution, and consumption would be completely disrupted. The severe physical damage from blast, fire, and radiation in the target countries would preclude the type of support that made recovery possible following World War II. The global breakdown of life-support, communications, transportation, financial, and other systems would compound the difficulties caused by food shortages in non-target countries. Long-term recovery would be uncertain.

Agricultural production and the survival of natural ecosystems would be threatened by a considerable reduction in sunlight, temperatures several degrees below normal, and the suppression of precipitation. These effects would be aggravated by chemical pollutants, an increase in ultra-violet radiation associated with ozone depletion, and the likely persistence of radioactive "hotspots." This sensitivity of agricultural systems and natural ecosystems to variations in temperature, precipitation, and light, means that the widespread impact of a nuclear exchange on the global climate would pose a severe threat to world food production. The prospect of widespread starvation as a consequence of a nuclear war would confront both target and non-target nations. The human impact would be exacerbated by an almost complete breakdown of health care in target countries and the likelihood of an increase in damaging ultra-violet radiation. The direct effects of a major nuclear exchange could kill millions: the indirect effects could kill billions.

New generations must understand what nuclear weapons do. They are not just an advanced form of weaponry: they have the power to decimate the natural environment that has sustained humanity since the beginning of time. Nuclear weapons:

- cause death and destruction;

- induce cancers, leukemia, keloids, and related afflictions;

- cause gastro-intestinal, cardiovascular, and related afflictions;

- continue for decades to induce health-related problems;

- cause congenital deformities, mental retardation, and genetic damage;

- could cause a nuclear winter;

- contaminate and destroy the food chain;

- imperil the eco-system;

- produce lethal levels of heat and blast;

- produce radiation and radioactive fallout;

- produce a disruptive electro-magnetic pulse;

- produce social disintegration;

- imperil all civilization;

- threaten human survival;

- wreak cultural devastation;

- threaten all life on the planet;

- irreversibly damage environmental and other rights of future generations;

- exterminate civilian populations;

- damage neighbouring states;

- produce psychological stress and fear syndromes.

The above descriptions of the overwhelming effects of nuclear weapons are not found in the general political and military literature on the subject. They were, however, emphasized by Judge Christopher Weeramantry of the World Court. The brutalities often tend to be hidden behind a veil of generalities, platitudes, and obfuscation. One of the favourite phrases of nuclear proponents is "unintended collateral damage": any civilian deaths from a nuclear bomb are unfortunate but unintended. Such phrases make a mockery of language. The very nature of nuclear weapons is to kill *massively*. A close and unvarnished examination of the technological leap represented by nuclear weapons is essential to an understanding of the multifarious threats to the human condition they pose. Nuclear weapons stand indicted in the court of world opinion. In the words of George Kennan, a distinguished American diplomat who originated the American "containment" policy towards the Soviet Union:

> The readiness to use nuclear weapons against other human beings — against people we do not know, whom we have never seen, and whose guilt or innocence it is not for us to establish — and, in doing so, to place in jeopardy the natural structure upon which all civilization rests, as though the safety and perceived interests of our own generation were more important than everything that has taken place or could take place in civilization: this is nothing less than a presumption, a blasphemy, an indignity — an indignity of monstrous dimensions — offered to God!

2

The Proliferation of Nuclear Weapons

In 1970, the Non-Proliferation Treaty (NPT) which obliged nations to negotiate nuclear disarmament, came into existence. At the time, the five declared nuclear states — the United States, the Soviet Union, Britain, France, and China — possessed 39,871 nuclear weapons. In 1995, on the 25th anniversary of the NPT, they possessed 40,640, most of them with a destructive capacity many times greater than the bomb that destroyed Hiroshima. How can it be said that the nuclear states are taking nuclear disarmament seriously?

At the height of the Cold War in 1986, the global nuclear stockpile rose to 70,298. Now the total is down: disarmament is occurring. The United States and Russia plan to enter a third round of Strategic Arms Reduction Talks (START III), where they intend to negotiate their strategic, long-range warheads down to 2,000-2,500 each by the end of 2007. But this figure includes only *deployed* strategic weapons, and when all other nuclear weapons — reserve, inactive, non-strategic, short-range, non-strategic spares, plus the nuclear arsenals of Britain, France, and China — are taken into consideration, the number of nuclear weapons remaining in the world in 2007 will be at least 16,924 (see next page).

This is a far cry from the disarmament the nuclear states claim is occurring. Since the negotiations on START III are dependent on the Russian Duma's ratification of START II, even this figure may not be achieved. The Duma, angry over NATO's expansion, is holding up the ratification of START II. The Russian leadership feels threatened by the determination of an expanded NATO (Poland, Hungary, and the Czech Republic will be added in 1999) to maintain nuclear weapons, though at reduced levels, as an "essential" component of Western security.

Global Nuclear Weapons							
1997				2007			
	Strategic Deployed	Non-Strategic	Reserve/Inactive	Total	Strategic Deployed	Non-Strategic	Reserve/Inactive	Total
United States	7,150	1,150	7,100	15,400	2,000-2,500	500	5,000-5,500	7,500-8,500
Russia	6,670	4,400	8,000-10,000	20,000-22,000	1,500-2,000	2,000	+/-5,000	8,500-9,000
United Kingdom	140	100	n.a.	240	140	n.a.	n.a.	+/- 140
France	384	65	n.a.	450	384	n.a.	n.a	+/- 384
China	149	246	n.a.	+/- 400	149	+/- 246	n.a.	+/- 400
	Grand Total 36,490-38,490				Grand Total 16,924-18,424			
n.a. = not available							
2007: Estimates for Russia, U.K, China and France							

The decline in nuclear numbers is what makes the public think the problem is going away. It is not. The nuclear states — the five permanent members of the Security Council — are determined to maintain their stocks because they are using them as the currency of power over the non-nuclear states. Power is at the core of the proliferation dilemma.

To understand the proliferation problem, we must look first at existing stocks.

The Five Declared Nuclear States

The United States

Having pioneered the development of the atomic bomb in 1945, the United States went on to produce about 70,000 warheads developed through 1,030 tests over a fifty-year period. Its current stockpile has about 8,300 operational warheads with a cumulative yield of some 2,000 megatons. Another 7,100 warheads are in reserve status or are waiting to be dismantled. Under current plans, Washington will keep at least 7,500 warheads, retain the three national laboratories that support warhead research and development, and decide on a consolidated production complex.

Although no new nuclear weapons have been produced through most of the 1990s, some existing warheads are being adapted for new roles. For example, the United States is deploying the new B61-11 (known as a "bunker-busting" nuclear weapon) designed to strike command bunkers buried hundreds of metres below the ground and other deeply buried targets. With a yield of somewhere between 300 tons and 300 kilotons, even in its "micro-nuke" setting, such an underground burst would create massive radioactive fallout. In 1996, Washington became the first to sign the Comprehensive Test Ban Treaty, which was supposed to end all nuclear testing in all environments for all time: yet a few months later, it began a series of "subcritical" underground tests to learn how to design more reliable and "survivable" nuclear weapons. Each year, Washington spends $20-$25 billion to operate and maintain its nuclear arsenal.

The United States points out that it has greatly reduced its number of nuclear weapons from its Cold War peak. This is a true statement, but its sub-text is a 1994 decision of a formal administration review of nuclear policy that it would maintain nuclear deterrence as American policy. Department of Defense testimony before a Congressional Committee in 1997 made clear that complete nuclear disarmament would only follow a process of general and complete disarmament:

> For the foreseeable future, we will continue to need a reliable and flexible nuclear deterrent — survivable against the most aggressive attack, under highly confidential constitutional command and control, and assured in its safety against both accident and unauthorized use.

Russia
Following the bombings of Hiroshima and Nagasaki, Soviet leader Josef Stalin ordered a crash program to provide the Soviets with atomic weapons in the shortest possible time. In 1949, by which time Washington had produced 170 nuclear weapons, the Soviets developed their first. The nuclear arms race was on. Over the following 46 years, the Soviets produced about 55,000 warheads, including some 1,000 used in 715 tests. In the mid-1980s, nuclear weapons were kept in more than 600 storage sites throughout the Soviet Union: that number is now down to 100 sites in Russia. Three republics — Ukraine, Belarus, and Khazakhstan — which had sizable numbers of Soviet nuclear weapons deployed on their territory, are now nuclear-free.

In 1986, Mikhail Gorbachev, newly installed as Soviet leader, put forward a comprehensive fifteen-year plan for the elimination of nuclear weapons. Later, at the United Nations, he renounced the use of force as an instrument of foreign policy. After Gorbachev fell from power, Boris Yeltsin went to a Security Council summit on January

31, 1992 and pledged to continue his predecessor's anti-nuclear-weapons policies. But by 1993, Russia had backed away from any innovative moves to eliminate nuclear weapons. It dropped its no-first-use pledge and began voting with the West at the U.N. to oppose resolutions proposing comprehensive nuclear disarmament. The Russian military leadership sees nuclear weapons as central to deterring both conventional and nuclear war. With NATO expanding, Russian hardliners argue that large stocks of nuclear weapons are needed to offset a conventional imbalance. (This is the same argument the West used to justify nuclear weapons during the Cold War, when it feared Soviet conventional superiority.) A limited number of new Russian warheads are being produced (for the SS-25 ICBM) to add to the current stockpile of...operational warheads, with more than 11,000 in reserve or awaiting dismantlement.

United Kingdom
The United Kingdom built its first nuclear weapon in 1953: its current stockpile has about 240 warheads of three types, with a cumulative yield of 45 megatons. Each Trident submarine has a killing capacity equivalent to 640 Hiroshima bombs. Under the Conservative government, the British missile program threatened limited nuclear strikes to defend vital interests, defined in a 1995 Defence White Paper as British trade, the sea routes used for it, raw materials from abroad, and overseas investments. Many expect the Labour government, elected in 1997, to review the country's nuclear policies, despite its initial exclusion of nuclear weapons from a review of defence policy.

France
French nuclear capability owes its origins to President Charles De Gaulle, for whom French possession of the bomb symbolized independence and a greater role in European and global affairs. Without a French bomb, De Gaulle felt the superpowers would carry on their two-way dialogue, taking little notice of the smaller nations. Starting in 1960, France began to produce air, sea, and land-based missiles, both strategic and tactical, and helped Israel build its nuclear weapons base. To the consternation of much of the world, in 1996 the Conservative government of President Jacques Chirac broke a testing moratorium instituted by his predecessor, François Mitterand. France continues to develop a selective nuclear capability directed against specific military forces or sensitive installations. Two new programs

are going ahead: the M-5 submarine-based strategic nuclear missile, and the more powerful *Air-Sol Moyenne Portee* air-launched nuclear missile. The current French stockpile numbers nearly 450 warheads of four types with a cumulative yield of 100 megatons.

China

The Chinese nuclear program started in 1955 with assistance from the Soviet Union. In time, the Chinese went ahead on their own and tested their first fission bomb in 1964. Another 44 tests followed through 1995, by which time the Chinese had produced their present arsenal of nearly 400 nuclear weapons with a cumulative yield of 400 megatons. At the United Nations, China regularly votes for negotiations on a time-bound program of nuclear disarmament. Meanwhile, it is working on several programs to modernize its forces. These include a new bomber, several new ballistic missiles, and nuclear submarines. And China is the world's biggest source for technology used by developing countries building ballistic missiles, chemical weapons, or nuclear bombs.

Threshold Countries

In addition to the five declared nuclear states, several others are considered to be of prime proliferation concern today. India, Pakistan, and Israel are "threshold" nuclear states, that is, they are widely understood to be capable of deploying nuclear arms quickly in a crisis, but have not openly admitted as much. None of the three has signed the NPT.

- India, which detonated a single nuclear test in 1974, is thought to have sufficient fissile material for 80 to 100 nuclear weapons. It has developed and deployed 150- to 250- kilometre range nuclear-capable missiles, known as the Prithvi, which could strike major targets throughout much of Pakistan. It must be assumed that India has designed a nuclear warhead for the Prithvi and has worked to develop even more powerful fission weapons and its own hydrogen bomb. Public opinion in India supports the acquisition of nuclear weaponry. Only a global, time-bound program for nuclear disarmament could convince the Indian government to forego the nuclear option.

- Pakistan secretly launched its nuclear program in 1972, with assistance from China, which supplied it with fissile material and nuclear device design. In 1983, an American State Department report declared that there was "unambiguous evidence that Pakistan is actively pursuing a nuclear weapons development program." Pakistan now has enough weapons-grade material to produce fifteen to twenty devices and has a variety of nuclear-capable aircraft, including American-supplied F-16s. It is also believed that Pakistan has received the nuclear-capable, short-range M-11 missile from China.

- Israel, with a ready arsenal of 100, and possibly as many as 200, nuclear weapons, is the most advanced of the three threshold nuclear powers. Experts believe it has deployed nuclear-capable missiles (the 660-km range Jericho I and the 1,500-km range Jericho II), that it has manufactured reliable nuclear warheads for these systems, and that it has developed highly efficient weapons that might be considerably more powerful than those used against Hiroshima and Nagasaki. Much of Israel's nuclear technology has come from France, which supplied it with a reactor and a plutonium extraction plant.

"High-Risk" Countries
There are a number of countries thought to be at "high risk" of being, or of soon becoming, capable of deploying nuclear weapons.

- Despite its extreme poverty, North Korea may possess the ability to deploy one, or possibly two, nuclear weapons using plutonium that Washington believes it produced in 1989 at a research reactor and reprocessing plant at Yongbyon. Although North Korea signed the NPT in 1985, it didn't permit international inspection until 1992, giving rise to the belief that technicians extracted enough plutonium to manufacture one or two nuclear weapons. North Korea possesses a variety of short-range, nuclear-capable ballistic missiles. Currently, its nuclear program is frozen under an agreement with the United States, in which, in return for international financing of two nuclear reactors by 2003, North Korea has pledged to dismantle nuclear weapons facilities and allow international inspection.

- Based on still-classified intelligence, the United States has declared that Iran has an active nuclear weapons development program under way and is making "unrelenting" efforts to buy the technology to make sophisticated ballistic missiles. So far, Iran is not known to have begun constructing any of the sensitive installations such a program would require, and it is thought to be five to ten years away from producing a first nuclear device. A vast smuggling network moving advanced weapons and parts from Russia to Iran has been uncovered. Iran has joined the NPT and all its known nuclear facilities are under international inspection.

• During the 1980s, Iraq, which is also a party to the NPT, built a massive and multi-faceted nuclear weapons infrastructure in violation of the Treaty. This was discovered by the U.N. Special Commission on Iraq, instituted to destroy Iraq's major weapons capabilities following the 1991 Gulf War. By then, Iraq was close to mastering the technology for producing weapon-grade uranium but had not perfected the design of a nuclear device. When the Gulf War began, Iraq appears to have been three to five years from producing a nuclear device.

• Although it has signed the NPT, Libya has pursued the development of weapons of mass destruction and ballistic missiles: its efforts to acquire chemical weapons in the late 1980s are well documented. Libya's nuclear development program is currently stalled and its nuclear research centre is under international inspection.

The Risk of Accidents

The news about nuclear weapons is not all bad: there have been some positive developments. South Africa began dismantling an arsenal of six nuclear weapons that had previously been undisclosed. Under dictator Nicolae Ceausescu, Romania pursued a nuclear weapons program in the 1980s, but the new government terminated it. Argentina and Brazil, which once pursued nuclear weapons development, have accepted comprehensive international inspections of their nuclear programs and established a bilateral nuclear inspection agency. Ukraine, Belarus, and Kazakhstan, three former Soviet republics that had 6,000 strategic and tactical nuclear weapons on their soil, have satisfactorily implemented agreements to transfer them to Russia.

Some developments provide hope that proliferation can be stopped, but political tensions in a number of areas may lead more states to conclude that they need nuclear weapons to flex their muscles. As internationally recognized expert Leonard S. Spector, Director of the Nuclear Non-Proliferation Project at the Carnegie Endowment for International Peace, points out:

> A number of generally more advanced non-nuclear-weapon States that are not considered proliferation threats today might re-examine their nuclear policies in the future. These States include Japan, South Korea, Taiwan, the States of Central and South Central Europe, Ukraine, Turkey, Syria and Egypt.
> The risk of use, intended or accidental, of nuclear weapons has always been high and is becoming more acute with the prospect of nuclear proliferation. From 1945 to 1980, about 100 accidents were reported that damaged nuclear weapons and might have caused unintended detonation. It is highly doubtful that a full accounting has been made of all such accidents and crises.

We do know of at least sixteen nuclear crises during the Cold War. The most fearsome was the 1962 Cuban missile crisis, when nuclear-armed missiles, supplied by the Soviet Union, were secretly installed in Cuba: unusually high numbers of American B-52 bombers were then ordered into the air, fully loaded with nuclear weapons. President Kennedy and General Secretary Khrushchov traded letters and threats before the crisis was resolved when the Soviets withdrew the Cuban missiles. Historians agree that the Cuban missile crisis brought the world to the brink of nuclear war. It also brought the reality of nuclear war home to the public and to the two superpower leaders.

In 1969, Washington implied it would use nuclear weapons to force North Vietnam to halt its operations in South Vietnam by its warning of "measures of the gravest consequence." Nuclear-armed B-52 bombers circled North Vietnam and Minuteman missiles were put on the highest state of readiness. A quarter of a million people protested in Washington, and the political leadership realized that the use of nuclear weapons would throw the American people into turmoil.

Some analysts hold that the most dangerous time in human history occurred in the 1983-85 period, when the United States developed a "first strike" system through the deployment of Pershing II and cruise missiles in five European countries. The flight time of these flat-tra-jectory missiles to Moscow was estimated at only six minutes. One Soviet response to this threat was to arm its submarines on patrol off the American east coast with flat-trajectory missiles of its own. Global nuclear war was on a hair trigger. Ongoing Soviet-American negotiations collapsed as both sides expanded their strategic arsenals. Washington began to develop the idea of a "shield," known as the Strategic Defence Initiative, to protect itself against Soviet missiles. These threatening plans of a nuclear holocaust — which could result from one side mis-reading the other — brought the possibility of mass devastation down to a six-minute window. Fortunately, the rise to power of Mikhail Gorbachev began a new period of eased tensions.

But in South Asia, another nuclear crisis developed. Investigative journalist Seymour Hersh has revealed that, in 1990, Pakistan and India faced off in a confrontation over Kashmir, a disputed territory over which they had already fought three wars. American intelligence was convinced that imminent war would go nuclear. The Americans, who had allowed Pakistan to assemble its nuclear arsenal with the aid of many millions of dollars' worth of restricted, high-tech materials, defused what looked to be inevitable warfare.

In addition to politically driven crises, there have been numerous false alarms and other mishaps that instantly sparked an increased level of nuclear readiness while the validity of information was being checked. For example, during the Cuban missile crisis, a Soviet satellite entered its parking orbit and exploded. Sir Bernard Lovell, director of the Jodrell Bank Observatory, later wrote: "The explosion of a Russian spacecraft ... led the U.S. to believe that the U.S.S.R. was launching a massive ICBM attack."

In that same period, a guard at a military installation in Duluth, Minnesota saw a figure climbing the security fence, shot at it, and activated a "sabotage alarm." This automatically set off other alarms at all bases in the area. At Volk Field, Wisconsin an alarm was wrongly wired, and the siren sounded ordering nuclear-armed F-106A interceptors to take off. Since the pilots were already in a state of high alert because of the Cuban crisis, they believed World War III had started. Immediate communication with Duluth revealed the error, but by this time, aircraft were starting down the runway. A car raced from the command centre and successfully signaled the aircraft to stop. The original intruder had been a bear.

In 1979, duty officers at four separate American command centres suddenly saw a pattern on their displays showing a large number of Soviet missiles in full-scale attack on the United States. During the next six minutes, emergency preparations for retaliation were taken. Air Force planes were launched. No attempt was made to use the Moscow-Washington "hot line," installed years earlier to forestall calamitous action based on faulty information. With commendable speed, NORAD officials were able to confirm that no missiles were in the air. The reason for the false alarm was an exercise tape running on the computer system.

Nuclear retentionists like to say that such accidents took place long ago and that modern systems now preclude such errors. In January, 1995, Russian early-warning radar detected an unexpected missile launch near Spitzbergen. The estimated flight time to Moscow was five minutes. The Russian President, the Defence Minister, and the Chief of Staff were informed. The early-warning and control and command systems switched to combat mode. Within five minutes, radar determined that the missile's impact point would be outside Russian borders. The missile was Norwegian, and was launched for scientific measurements. A few days earlier, Norway had notified 35 countries, including Russia, that the launch was planned. Information had apparently been sent to the Russian Defence Ministry, but failed to reach on-duty personnel.

The possibility of an actual progression to nuclear war on any one of these occasions may have been small, due to "fail-safe" features in the warning and launch systems or to responsible action by those in the chain of command when the fail-safe features failed. However, the accumulation of small probabilities of disaster adds up to serious danger. The command, communication, and control systems of the United States and the Soviet Union during the Cold War were undoubtedly firm. That errors could occur even in reliable systems points out the risk of multiple mistakes in the systems of states that might acquire nuclear weapons in the future.

The unauthorized acquisition of a nuclear weapon poses even greater risks. From time to time alarmist headlines announce that terrorists will soon be able to threaten to use a nuclear device. The growing evidence of nuclear smuggling from the former Soviet Union, the rapid growth of civilian plutonium stockpiles in Europe and Japan, and the truck-bomb attacks on the World Trade Center in New York, the Federal Building in Oklahoma City, and the American Army barracks in Saudi Arabia all have ominous implications for nuclear terrorism. Since the fall of 1992, at least five serious thefts of weapon-usable material, three involving highly enriched uranium and two of plutonium, have been intercepted. In July, 1997, the FBI charged two Lithuanians in Miami with attempting to sell munitions, anti-aircraft missiles, and even tactical nuclear weapons. Most of these clandestine materials were stolen from Russian nuclear facilities.

It would be possible for a terrorist group to produce a basic nuclear device, but the levels of expertise and materials needed to do so suggest that a random band of activists wouldn't be capable of such an enterprise: it would more likely be a state-sponsored enterprise. The idea that nuclear weapons can be easily produced is countered by the fact that a number of countries have unsuccessfully tried, with tremendous investments of personnel and resources, to build them. Even after years of effort, Iraq was unable, up to its defeat in 1991, to produce a functioning nuclear weapon.

Nonetheless, the fact that clandestine research has been continuing, despite international safeguards, reveals the ongoing danger of "breakout." Just because it is more difficult to construct a nuclear device than is sometimes inferred is no reason for complacency. Under the sponsorship of a malevolent regime, a group of terrorists could be dispatched anywhere to acquire material and build a bomb.

The Nuclear Control Institute of Washington, D.C. holds that the best defence against nuclear terrorism and proliferation is to end civilian commerce in plutonium and bomb-grade uranium, and to reduce military stocks of these materials as soon as possible. Since civilian use of plutonium is not likely to end, for a long time, a rigid tightening of the system of international safeguards is our best defence against nuclear terrorism. But such tightening will only work in the context of a global ban on the production of all fissile material for bombs and the elimination of nuclear weapons to stop the demand for such material.

The Effect of Military Expenditures

The sheer cost of nuclear weapons is staggering. Since work first began on the Manhattan Project, which developed the atomic bomb in World War II, the American nuclear arsenal has cost $4 trillion (in 1995 dollars). At least another $4 trillion has been spent by the other four acknowledged nuclear powers to develop, produce, and maintain their nuclear stocks. Nuclear weapons account for one-quarter to one-third of all military spending by the nuclear powers since World War II.

The costs of dismantling stocks must now be added to this total of $8 trillion spent so far by the nuclear states on nuclear weapons. Dismantling of nuclear weapons and storage of nuclear fuels will cost the United States and Russia at least $50 billion, but perhaps as much as $1 trillion, with the clean-up of military nuclear facilities estimated at an additional $400 billion. In the end, the cost of environmental remediation and waste management will probably exceed the cost of building the nuclear warheads in the first place. Russia cannot afford such costs, and its aging nuclear submarine fleet poses an immense environmental hazard. In the early 1990s, Washington, through the Cooperative Threat Reduction Act, started underwriting Russian dismantling at a cost of $400 million a year, a sum later cut as a result of Congressional opposition. Disarmament turns out to be costly.

The costs of nuclear weapons must be seen in the context of overall military expenditures. The world's governments spend more than $800 billion a year to support military forces of more than 27,000,000 soldiers. This is a decline of 31 percent in spending since the 1987 Cold War high of $1.26 trillion. But 80 percent of this decline came from the sharp drop in spending by the former Warsaw Pact nations. Despite the end of the Cold War, developed nations other than the East European countries spend only ten percent less than they did in 1987. Military expenditures of the NATO countries are now more than ten times those of the former Warsaw Pact countries. Not only are the developed countries big military spenders (accounting for 75 percent of the world's military spending) they are also responsible for 90 percent of the $22-billion annual arms trade. The dangerous global proliferation of conventional arms and weapons technology has helped to incite and prolong the dozens of major armed conflicts raging around the world in the 1990s.

For their part, the developing countries spend about $220 billion on armed forces each year. This is a tremendous drain on these nations' already limited resources: new weapons and larger armies mean there is less to invest in health, education, economic development, and other urgent social needs of large and vulnerable populations. Some 1.3 billion people are so poor they cannot meet their basic needs for food and shelter. Poverty is growing as fast as population. About 60 percent of humanity lives on less than U.S.$2 per day. Despite some remarkable successes in human development in some fast-growing economies, more than 100 countries are worse off today than they were fifteen years ago. Each year, 13 to 18 million people, mostly children, die from hunger and other poverty-related causes.

Sustainable development requires huge investments in scientific research, technological development, education and training, infrastructure development, and the transfer of technology. Such investments are urgently needed to stop the poisoning of the atmosphere and the depletion of the earth's biological riches — the forests, wetlands, and plant and animal species now under attack. But the goals of sustainable development set out in the 1992 Earth Summit's major document, Agenda 21, are blocked by continued political inertia, which allows continued high military spending to remain unchecked. The Committee on Sustainable Development, an international non-governmental organization (NGO) has urged governments to reduce military expenditures by five percent per year for five years, re-directing these funds to sustainable development. But the opposite is happening. Arms merchants will soon make new billions of dollars from NATO's expansion, as new members re-equip to Western standards. A 1997 U.N.-sponsored Earth Summit in New York, intended to renew the 1992 global commitment to sustainable development, was an abject failure. It could not agree on the wording of a political statement, and did not even consider the transfer of military funds to sustainable development.

The Indian-Pakistani enmity illustrates dramatically the human cost of escalating arms expenditures. Military spending in South Asia, led by India and Pakistan, is rising dramatically, and that region is now one of the most militarized in the world. At great cost, South Asian countries are acquiring a range of modern weapons, particularly jet fighters, submarines, and missiles. India ranks first in the world in total arms imports, Pakistan tenth. With basic social services severely under-funded in both countries, their rising military burdens continue to impose prohibitive social and economic costs to their people. Education and health spending is slashed to pay for weapons. Aside from sub-Saharan Africa, South Asia is fast emerging as the poorest, the most illiterate, the most malnourished, indeed, the most deprived region in the world. Yet it continues to invest more in arms than in uplifting its people. Although they have now entered a period of dialogue, India and Pakistan's maintenance of nuclear weapons is both a moral scandal and a growing danger to the world.

Yet more danger lies ahead, with the prospect of nuclear-powered battle stations in space. Although the 1967 Outer Space Treaty bans nuclear weapons in outer space, the use of nuclear energy is planned for new weapons programs in space. The United States is already well advanced in the development of its Cassini rocket, which carries 72.3 pounds of plutonium-235 fuel, the largest amount ever used in space. This plutonium is intended to power radioisotope thermal generators to run instruments on both military and civilian satellites. Scientists are working to develop pure fusion and other weapons that can beam microwaves, at immense power levels, to disable targets in space or on the ground.

Nuclear technology is the basis of these advanced military space projects. In 1996, the U.S. Air Force Advisory Board said: "In the next two decades, new technologies will allow the fielding of space-based weapons of devastating effectiveness to deliver energy and mass as force projection in tactical and strategic conflict." Nuclear power in space is needed to supply energy for these weapons. Even if solar power could be harnessed for military use, it does not provide the profit of nuclear energy for the major weapons corporations that are driving this new development. Space is the new nuclear market.

A worldwide coalition, the Global Network Against Weapons and Nuclear Power in Space, is trying to stop the nuclearization of outer space. But no technological revolution in weaponry has yet been stopped. The United Nations has been trying for years to ensure that the development of space would be used only for peaceful purposes. But the General Assembly has not yet been able to agree even on empowering a committee to conduct negotiations to prevent an arms race in space. As long as the militarist mentality prevails that nuclear weapons are okay for the powerful, there is little likelihood of keeping wars out of space.

3

Jeopardizing the Non-Proliferation Treaty

The Non-Proliferation Treaty is central to the ability of the world community to develop peacefully as we journey into the Third Millennium. Now signed by 186 countries, it is at the heart of global efforts to reduce nuclear weapons to zero. But the NPT's central provision, which calls for good-faith negotiations on nuclear disarmament, is not being carried out, and, in fact, the Treaty itself is in jeopardy.

The media and the public are, for the most part, oblivious to the dangers of the proliferation of nuclear weapons because they have been engrossed by the bilateral nuclear negotiations between the Soviet Union (now Russia) and the United States. While it is true that the two major powers account for 97 percent of all nuclear weapons in existence, it is the NPT that is supposed to stop their proliferation to other countries. Success or failure in halting proliferation will have a much greater effect on the future of humanity than the actual numbers of weapons possessed by the Big Two.

From its very first resolution, the United Nations has consistently addressed the arms issue, giving special attention to the haunting problems of nuclear escalation. After the adoption in 1961 of framework principles for general and complete disarmament under strict and effective international control, and after the successful negotiations in 1963 leading to the Partial Nuclear Test Ban Treaty, the (then) eighteen-nation Committee on Disarmament turned its attention to negotiations on an international treaty to stop the proliferation of nuclear weapons.

By 1968, the NPT, consisting of eleven articles and twelve preambular paragraphs, was ready for adoption by the General Assembly.

It came into force for a 25-year period on March 5, 1970, when the requisite 40 signatory states had ratified it.

Two principles are of fundamental importance in the NPT. One is that the spread of nuclear weapons undermines international peace and security; the second is that the peaceful use of nuclear energy should be made universally available. Since the U.N. Charter is, for all practical purposes, a pre-atomic-age document, the NPT literally supplements the Charter in addressing problems of the atom and development. The NPT involves five commitments: acceptance of a political and moral norm against the possession of nuclear weapons; an obligation to eliminate existing stocks; international cooperation in the peaceful uses of energy; special assistance to developing countries; and measures to ensure a world free of nuclear weapons. In essence, the NPT promised a world in which nuclear weapons would be eliminated and technological cooperation for development would be widespread.

The NPT certainly did not bless the existence of nuclear weapons: it simply accepted the basic fact that the United States, the Soviet Union, Britain, France, and China possessed them. These five entered the NPT as Nuclear Weapons States (NWS). (The first three entered immediately. China and France signed the Treaty in 1992). All other States would join the NPT as Non-Nuclear Weapons States (NNWS).

Under Article I, NWS parties to the Treaty agree to refrain from transferring nuclear weapons to any recipient. Similarly, under Article II, NNWS undertake not to receive or control any nuclear weapons.

Article III obliges the NNWS to accept the safeguards of the International Atomic Energy Agency (IAEA) "with a view to preventing diversion of nuclear energy from peaceful uses to nuclear weapons or other nuclear explosive devices." All signatories must refrain from providing fissionable and related material to any NNWS unless it is safeguarded.

Article IV emphasizes the universal right to the development of nuclear energy for peaceful purposes and the need for cooperation "with due consideration for the needs of the developing areas of the world." Article V deals with nuclear test explosions by the NWS, but it is now a dead letter, since the Comprehensive Test Ban Treaty (CTBT), adopted in 1996, prohibits all nuclear test explosions.

The centrepiece of the NPT is Article VI, which states in its entirety:

> Each of the Parties to the Treaty undertakes to pursue nego-
> tiations in good faith on effective measures relating to ces-
> sation of the nuclear arms race at an early date and to nuclear
> disarmament, and on a treaty on general and complete dis-
> armament under strict and effective international control.

This language underlines the spirit of the Treaty's Preamble, which
speaks of the need to ease international tensions and so make it easier
to end the production of nuclear weapons and to eliminate them from
national arsenals, along with their delivery systems. The Preamble
adds that states, in accordance with the U.N. Charter, must refrain
from the threat or use of force: international peace and security are
to be promoted "with the least diversion for armaments of the world's
human and economic resources."

Although references to Article VI frequently involve the obligations of the NWS, the text actually addresses all parties. It is clearly
the language of compromise. The ongoing battle over the effectiveness of the NPT centres on semantics. Many NNWS argue that the
primary obligation is on the NWS to get rid of nuclear weapons, an
act which would be instrumental in advancing general disarmament.
For their part, the NWS hold that they have stopped the nuclear arms
race, and that further progress toward their elimination is contingent
on the easing of international tensions, which would then allow
progress on general disarmament. In this larger goal, say the NWS,
the NNWS have their responsibility.

Article VII promotes nuclear-weapon-free zones. There are five
such regional treaties embracing 114 countries and more than half
the earth's mass: the 1959 Antarctic Treaty; the 1967 Treaty of
Tlatelolco covers a vast territory throughout Latin America and the
Caribbean; the 1985 Treaty of Rarotonga covers much of the South
Pacific; the 1995 Treaty of Bangkok takes in South-East Asia; the
1996 Treaty of Pelindaba extends throughout Africa.

Article VIII provides for a five-year review process. At the 1975
and 1985 reviews, a final declaration, endorsing the Treaty, was
agreed upon. At the 1980, 1990, and 1995 reviews, no consensus was
possible. Article IX defines the ratification process. Article X allows
for withdrawal from the Treaty on three-months notice if a party
decides that extraordinary events "have jeopardized the supreme
interests of its country." Article XI establishes the United States, the
United Kingdom, and the Soviet Union (Russia) as the three deposi-
tory states.

The NPT Indefinitely Extended

As 1995 loomed, many states feared that an indefinite extension of the NPT would be treated by the NWS as a *de facto* legitimization of the status quo, namely that the NWS could keep their nuclear weapons pending such a dramatic improvement in world conditions that full-scale disarmament would be viable. China had already committed itself to negotiations on a time-bound program for nuclear disarmament. The other four NWS addressed the problem of their credibility a few days before the 1995 Review Conference opened:

> We solemnly reaffirm our commitment, as stated in Article VI, to pursue negotiations in good faith on effective measures relating to nuclear disarmament, which remains our ultimate goal.

"Ultimate" is the key word in this sentence. "Ultimate" means "eventual" or "last," and conveys the idea of remoteness in time or space. Thus, while seeking to give assurances of their sincerity, the NWS were criticized for giving themselves an unspecified period of time to keep their nuclear weapons. This returned the argument to its essential counterpoint and fed the belief that indefinite extension of the NPT would perpetuate, at least well into the next century, the division of the world into two classes.

Knowing that, short of a commitment to time-bound disarmament, the issue was unresolvable, and fearing a weakened treaty as a result of a vote, the United States, Britain, and France launched a worldwide campaign to convince countries, particularly those over whom they retained some economic leverage, that indefinite and unconditional extension was in everyone's best interests. On the eve of the Review Conference, vote-counters estimated that, in a vote, indefinite extension would likely win.

The President of the Conference, Ambassador Jayantha Dhanapala of Sri Lanka, crafted a "package" deal made up of three resolutions dealing with a strengthened review process, a set of Principles and Objectives, and an indefinite extension of the Treaty. Having obtained assurances from the dissenters that they would not ask for a vote (which they would have lost), Dhanapala declared that the package of three resolutions was "adopted without a vote." It thus became politically (some argue also legally) binding. Thirteen states denounced the action, but the deal was done.

When the delegates turned to the Final Declaration of the Conference, rancor again broke out, this time centred on the refusal of the NWS to commit themselves to comprehensive negotiations. Despite indefinite extension, no agreement was possible on the implementation of the Treaty's central obligation, Article VI.

The strengthened review process included the holding of annual preparatory meetings, starting in 1997, prior to each five-year review. At the 1997 meeting preparing for the 2000 review, the three Western NWS insisted on regional stability as a pre-condition for nuclear disarmament. They made clear they have no intention, in the foreseeable future, of entering into comprehensive negotiations. Canada explicitly rejected the NWS contention that nuclear disarmament can be achieved only when complete disarmament is accomplished, but found itself in a minority position in the Western group, dominated by the United States, Britain, and France. The non-aligned movement once again called for negotiations leading to the "complete elimination of nuclear weapons within a specified framework of time." The impasse continues.

The 61-nation Conference on Disarmament (the permanent multilateral disarmament negotiating forum, which operates from Geneva) was to complete, no later than 1996, a universal and effectively verifiable Comprehensive Nuclear Test Ban Treaty (CTBT). This was accomplished, but the problems surrounding the negotiations illustrate why an unequivocal commitment to the elimination of nuclear weapons is necessary.

When the long-awaited negotiations for a CTBT began, worldwide expectations rose that, finally, a treaty would end all nuclear tests, by all countries, in all environments, for all time. While the CTBT is a major political step forward by the international community, stopping nuclear tests *does not* equal nuclear disarmament. It does nothing to reduce the nuclear weapons still in existence. For the technologically advanced, tests are no longer needed to maintain nuclear weapons stocks. Thus, the CTBT draft was seen by some as a non-proliferation measure, not a disarmament measure: it would prohibit less technologically advanced states from testing, while doing nothing to disarm those who already possess nuclear weapons.

India found this particularly offensive and unacceptable, and it blocked passage of the CTBT in the consensus-driven Conference on Disarmament. Just as India has always refused to join the NPT on the grounds that it is essentially a discriminatory document — it permits the nuclear states to retain their armaments while proscribing nuclear weapons for anyone else — so too it refused to join the CTBT. India and many other nations want a global ban on nuclear weapons. (At the U.N. Third Special Session on Disarmament in 1988, Rajiv Gandhi, then India's Prime Minister, proposed a fifteen-year plan for a nuclear weapon-free world: it was rebuffed by the Western states.)

An international treaty normally designates merely the number of states that must ratify it before it enters into force, not their names. But in the case of the CTBT, the Western states insisted that it would have to be ratified by all forty-four nations possessing nuclear reactors. This was intended to put India on the spot. When negotiations broke down, the operation was shifted to the U.N. General Assembly, which adopted the draft text. India stated that it would not sign the CTBT and hence not ratify it. Pakistan and North Korea are the only other states of the forty-four that have not signed it. If they maintain their opposition, the CTBT (barring later amendments) will never be ratified. While India was blamed for the impasse, India was not the cause of the CTBT problem: rather, its position underlines the global nuclear disarmament stalemate. The core problem of meeting the requirements of the NPT remain. Though India has been accused of hypocrisy by the West in calling for a global ban while keeping its own nuclear options open, the hypocrisy lies more in the Western camp, which extended the NPT but refused negotiations.

The Conference on Disarmament was called upon to bring to an "early conclusion" negotiations on a non-discriminatory and universally applicable convention barring the production of fissile material for nuclear weapons or other explosive devices. The Western NWS want such a ban to apply only to future production, since they already have huge stocks of fissile material and are not producing any more. Leading non-aligned countries want negotiations to include existing stocks. While many non-aligned countries are willing to proceed with negotiations on future production only, they want such a concession to be matched by a NWS agreement to set up a committee in the Conference on Disarmament to at least discuss, if not negotiate, a program for nuclear disarmament.

The Principles and Objectives agreed to in the 1995 "package" called for the establishment of more nuclear-weapon-free zones. At the U.N. General Assembly in 1996, eighty countries, led by Brazil and New Zealand, tried to strengthen the five zones, principally in the southern hemisphere, by introducing a resolution consolidating their status. The United States and Britain put pressure on NATO and would-be NATO countries to oppose this resolution on the grounds that it would threaten rights of passage of the NWS through the proposed consolidated zone. Its sponsors rejoined that existing international law relating to rights of passage through maritime space would prevail. The Western NWS would not budge.

The 1995 Principles and Objectives also addressed the need to strengthen security assurances. A security assurance is any type of assistance a state receives or is promised from an outside source that contributes to its security. In the nuclear field, assurances fall into two broad categories: positive assurances are those that contribute to a state's ability to defend itself against attack; negative assurances are promises not to attack a state. On the eve of the 1995 NPT Review Conference, the NWS adopted a Security Council resolution which stated that a country may request "urgent action" by the Security Council in the investigation of disputes, humanitarian assistance, and compensation from an aggressor. The resolution, however, is not legally binding, and the NWS continue to resist making it so. Also, the NNWS want the nuclear states to pledge no-first-use of nuclear weapons (only China has done so). Their reluctance further weakens their claim to be adhering to the NPT.

The Dilemma of Nuclear Power

The Principles and Objectives also called for IAEA's inspection capability to be increased. From the dawn of the nuclear age, nuclear power has been recognized as a "dual-use" technology. The same nuclear reactors that give bombs their destructive force of many thousands of tons of high explosive can, when harnessed in a controlled fashion, produce energy for peaceful purposes. The challenge is to prevent the proliferation of nuclear weapons while at the same time permitting countries to peacefully develop nuclear energy.

Today, nuclear power accounts for about five percent of the world's energy, and about fifteen percent of its electricity. Nuclear energy could replace fossil-fuel generation of electricity in many parts of the world and even lead to massive desalination programs that could provide safe drinking water. But, generally acceptable responses must be found to address concerns such as reactor safety, radioactive waste transport and disposal, and the proliferation of nuclear weapons.

The fight over the efficacy of nuclear energy is intense. The nuclear industry contends that the only way the electricity needs of the multiplying billions in the developing world can be met over the next quarter century is through nuclear power. Even conservation measures in the industrialized countries and increased reliance on renewable energy sources would not satisfy the coming demand for energy. Fossil fuels already pollute the atmosphere and contribute to global warming: besides, two-thirds of the world's oil reserves are located in the Middle East, which is constantly vulnerable to political change. Energy needs and environmental degradation will be the supreme security issue of the twenty-first century, in this view. Since nuclear energy doesn't add to the greenhouse effect, doesn't contribute to acid rain, and doesn't deplete the ozone layer, its substantial advantages suggest it could play a far more important role in the future than it does now.

The opposite view is expressed by such bodies as the Nuclear Control Institute and the Lawyers' Committee on Nuclear Policy, which hold that nuclear energy creates a legacy of serious long-lasting environmental and health problems, and that it enables proliferation of nuclear weapons. The 1986 accident at Chernobyl released 300 times the radiation let loose by the Hiroshima bomb, and it contaminated adjoining countries. In addition to health hazards, the problem of safe disposal of radioactive waste for up to 250,000 years is overwhelming. There is no known way of storing this waste safely and securely for such a long period. Opponents of nuclear energy hold that it is irresponsible to keep producing this waste before scientists have developed storage methods and trans-civilization communication tools that could overcome these problems.

Finally, opponents believe that safeguards against the diversion of nuclear materials to weapons programs are too weak. Iraq and North Korea, which re-directed assistance received for nuclear energy into nuclear-weapons programs, are cases in point. They were actually spotted by international inspection, but South Africa produced nuclear weapons without detection.

The NPT requires that "safeguards" be applied by IAEA, the world's nuclear watchdog. If nuclear material is diverted from a peaceful nuclear program for weapons purposes, IAEA is supposed to detect it in time to permit an international response before the diverted material is made into bombs. Many nations, relying on IAEA to deter diversions by means of such "timely detection," accept the use of weapons-quality nuclear fuel (plutonium and highly enriched uranium) for energy production as a legitimate use of "atoms for peace."

IAEA has been under-funded and under-staffed for years. With civilian plutonium stocks set to skyrocket (from 140 tons in 1995 to 250 tons in 2005) and the growing dangers of leakage and theft, IAEA has received the backing of the international community for a strengthened safeguards program. This aims to better equip it to detect clandestine nuclear activity through state-of-the-art technologies, to trace activity through samples taken from the environment, and to remotely operate surveillance systems at key locations in inspected states. Though this is an advance, it has not eliminated the proliferation threat posed by nuclear energy.

If, in the long run, nuclear power comes to produce an even more significant proportion of world energy, the safeguarding of weapons-usable materials will become still more daunting. A nuclear explosive can be made with less than ten kilograms of plutonium, while a 1,000 megawatt power reactor produces more than 200 kilograms of plutonium per year. It is difficult to imagine human institutions capable of safeguarding these plutonium flows against occasional diversions of significant quantities to nuclear weapons.

To buttress IAEA safeguards, several multilateral groups have been formed to control the export of equipment and material that might be used in the production of weapons of mass destruction. One such organization, made up of the Western nuclear powers and other countries involved in the production of nuclear energy, is the Nuclear Suppliers Group (also known as the London Group) which requires importers of nuclear technology to accept IAEA monitoring of their entire nuclear programs. It focusses on a "trigger list" of items, such as enrichment, re-processing, and heavy-water production. This leaves China as the only supplier of nuclear technology not requiring "full-scope safeguards" as a condition of sale. As a general position, the non-aligned states object to *ad hoc* export-control groups, since they could impede the economic and social progress of developing countries. They argue consistently that they have an "inalienable right" to the benefits of the peaceful use of nuclear energy.

In fact, that "inalienable right" to nuclear energy was written into the NPT, and many developing countries keep insisting on their right to receive from developed countries "the fullest possible exchange of equipment, materials and scientific and technological information for the peaceful uses of nuclear energy." When the NPT was negotiated, nuclear power was a new technology, and there was widespread optimism in the possibilities of this largely untried energy source. It was expected to be "clean, cheap, and safe," but the experience of the following decades has proven otherwise, as nuclear programs have run up enormous debts, ever-accumulating quantities of radioactive waste await safe disposal, and a legacy of health and environmental problems has emerged. A sober assessment of the problems stemming from nuclear power has led the United Nations Development Programme to conclude that nuclear power "is not a necessary component of the energy supply system in a world where emphasis is given to the efficient use of energy and innovation in energy supply technologies."

However, the ability to move towards a sustainable energy future depends on coalitions around common development, economic, technological, and energy issues. These coalitions are only beginning to develop, and the governments of developed countries have refused to put more than marginal amounts of money into sustainable development. As Greenpeace puts it directly: "The profits of the commercial nuclear industry appear to have been put ahead of non-proliferation objectives." A number of non-governmental organizations hold that, given the development of alternate sources of energy and IAEA's inability to completely safeguard plutonium, the prudent course would be for nations to ban the civilian use of plutonium. Moreover, some add, the abolition of nuclear weapons cannot be secured until all nuclear reactors are shut down.

Since so many governments want either to buy or sell nuclear energy, there is little discussion of the merits of nuclear energy at NPT meetings, where debates continue to centre around the meaning of the common pledge to pursue with determination "systematic and progressive efforts to reduce nuclear weapons globally." After the acrimony of the 1995 Review and Extension Conference, Ambassador Dhanapala warned:

> Any departure from the sincere implementation of the decisions will lead not only to cynicism over the freedom and democratization of the post-Cold War order but also to a dangerous build-up of dissatisfaction amongst a majority of Treaty parties, who could at any moment invoke their rights under Article 10:1 and leave the Treaty.

Since then, Mexico, testifying before the World Court, has said that if the disarmament obligations of the NPT are not met, "We would need to revise our continuation as party to the Treaty." Mexico warned:

As a country, we are not prepared under any circumstances to accept a monopoly in the possession of nuclear weapons or to allow the modernization of these devices through tests whose legality we also respectfully question.

Three days after the 1997 NPT preparatory committee meeting, India, watching from the sidelines, warned the U.N.:

The stubborn position of nuclear-weapon States has paralyzed the debate on nuclear disarmament. The window of opportunity opened at the end of the Cold War is closing.

PART TWO

Towards a
Nuclear-Weapon-Free World

4

The World Court's
Legal Challenge

The legal battle against nuclear weapons has entered a new phase.

Recognizing that civilians needed more protection from the new weapons of warfare, in 1949 the International Committee of the Red Cross revised the Geneva Convention on the laws of war and began advancing the idea that its general principles should apply to nuclear weapons. A former Irish Foreign Minister, Sean MacBride, became President of the International Peace Bureau, a worldwide network of peace activists founded in 1892, and, in 1974, won the Nobel Peace Prize for his work in human rights. MacBride gathered together a growing number of international lawyers who began to write about nuclear issues and international law. His work bore fruit in 1985 when he chaired the London Nuclear Warfare Tribunal, which concluded that "current and planned [nuclear] weapons developments, strategies and deployments violate the basic rules and principles of international law." MacBride launched a "Lawyers' Appeal" for the prohibition of nuclear weapons. His hope was to present it to the U.N. General Assembly, "which is empowered to request the International Court of Justice [the World Court] to give an opinion as to the validity of our declaration." Although MacBride died in 1988, by 1992 the Appeal had been signed by 11,000 lawyers from fifty-six countries.

Another non-governmental initiative started in New Zealand when a retired Christchurch magistrate, Harold Evans, compiled into an open letter the opinions of six leading international jurists, including Richard Falk, a prominent American lawyer, and Christopher Weeramantry of Sri Lanka, later to become a member of the World Court. Evans sent the letter to the prime ministers of Australia and New Zealand, challenging them to sponsor a U.N. resolution to seek a World Court opinion on "the legality or otherwise of nuclear weaponry." Though both governments declined, a campaign was started by Kate Dewes and Alyn Ware, two New Zealand activists, to mobilize citizen support for Evans' challenge. With the Cold War worsening as the 1980s progressed, more and more people in North America and Western Europe — religious leaders, academics, jurists, members of professional associations, and community activists — protested the escalating manufacture, testing, and deployment of nuclear weapons. Three principal groups, the International Association of Lawyers Against Nuclear Arms, the International Physicians for the Prevention of Nuclear War (awarded the Nobel Peace Prize in 1985 for its efforts to prevent nuclear war), and the International Peace Bureau, which won the same award way back in 1910, joined forces in 1992 to launch the World Court Project. Its object was to get an "Advisory Opinion" from the Court on the legality of nuclear weapons.

The World Court is the principal judicial organ of the United Nations. Sitting at the Peace Palace in the Hague, it has a dual role: to settle legal disputes submitted to it by states in accordance with international law, and to give Advisory Opinions on legal questions referred to it by the U.N. General Assembly, the Security Council, or specialized U.N. agencies. The Court is composed of fifteen judges[*] elected by the U.N. to nine-year terms of office.

Ordinarily, one judge from each of the five permanent members of the Security Council sits on the bench, although all judges are sworn to act independently. The Court has jurisdiction in disputed cases only when the parties involved agree to it. Advisory Opinions are consultative in character and are not binding.

Two questions were sent to the Court. The first was a resolution promoted by the International Physicians For the Prevention of Nuclear War at the 1992 assembly of the World Health Organization (WHO) which asked the World Court:

> In view of the health and environmental effects, would the use of nuclear weapons by a State in war or other armed conflict be a breach of its obligations under international law including the WHO constitution?

---

[*]   Because a Venezuelan judge died on the eve of the World Court hearings on nuclear weapons, its President, Mohammed Bedjaoui of Algeria, was authorized to cast a tie-breaking vote. This, in fact, happened.

Arguments by the Western nuclear states and their allies that WHO lacked the competence to ask this question were countered by the fact that WHO had been investigating the health and environmental effects of nuclear weapons since 1981. After intense lobbying by both sides, the WHO assembly adopted the resolution in 1993 by 73 votes to 40, with 10 abstentions. The question went forward, and the Court invited states to make submissions.

At the same time, an American group, Lawyers' Committee on Nuclear Policy, approached several U.N. missions in New York to get a similar resolution passed in the General Assembly. Zimbabwe announced its support and took the issue to the 111-nation Non-Aligned Movement, which then introduced a resolution urgently asking the World Court to render an Advisory Opinion on this second question:

Is the threat or use of nuclear weapons in any circumstance permitted under international law?

In strengthening the WHO question, the sponsors of this resolution were directly challenging the legality of the doctrine of nuclear deterrence. The Western nuclear states, fearing that a decision that nuclear weapons are illegal would undermine their basic military doctrine and also challenge their privileged status as permanent members of the Security Council, began intensive lobbying against the resolution. The United States, Britain, and France made diplomatic forays to many non-aligned capitals, threatening reductions in trade and aid if the resolution was not opposed. Meanwhile, non-governmental organizations lobbied diplomats in U.N. corridors to support the resolution. Experienced diplomats said the extreme reaction of the three Western nuclear states amounted to hysteria; the non-aligned movement buckled, and the resolution was withdrawn.

But the next year, 1994, the resolution was re-introduced. London claimed the resolution risked "being seen as a deliberate attempt to exert pressure over the Court to prejudice its response [to the WHO question ... It] can do nothing to further global peace and security." France said, "It is a blatant violation of the U.N. Charter. It goes against the law. It goes against reason ..." This time the resolution was put to a vote and it carried, 77 to 33, with 21 abstentions and 53 not voting. New Zealand voted in favour: Canada, Norway, Japan, Australia, and Ireland abstained. The solid Western opposition was broken. The resolution went forward to the General Assembly, which usually rubber-stamps committee resolutions. The Western nuclear states re-launched their opposition: activists of the World Court Project intensified their lobbying. The vote held. William Epstein, a former Director of the U.N.'s Disarmament Office, described the scene as "the most exciting night in the U.N. in 30 years." Yet there was almost no coverage of the drama in the Western media.

The World Court decided to examine both questions at the same time, and it set aside a two-week period in late 1995 for oral hearings in the Hague.

The Finding of the World Court

One of the first Russian writers on international law, Frederic de Martens (1845-1909) helped draft the Hague Convention, which has a clause stipulating that, until the drafting of a more complete code of the laws of war, people remain under the protection of the principles of the law of nations "as they result from the usages established among civilized peoples, from the laws of humanity, and the dictates of the public conscience." Leaders of the World Court Project hit on the idea of developing public support by using this clause from the 1907 Hague Convention as an individual "Declaration of Public Conscience." The concept of ordinary citizens signing personal Declarations of Conscience on a question of international law was novel. Only World Court judges could decide the legal status of nuclear weapons, but now ordinary citizens had a way to express their views. These Declarations of Public Conscience, signed by 170,000 people in Western countries and 3.3 million people in Japan, were presented to the Court by a delegation representing 700 non-governmental organizations.

The case turned out to be the largest in the Court's history. Of the forty-three governments submitting written opinions, two-thirds held that nuclear weapons were illegal under international law. Twenty-two nations gave oral testimony, most expressing the view that nuclear weapons are illegal. WHO argued that it is impossible to plan adequately for the utterly devastating effects of a nuclear war. Thus, a "public health" prevention strategy has to be developed. Just as smallpox, domestic violence, and drug trafficking can be characterized as public health issues, so too can nuclear weapons. One way to foster prevention is to question the legality of the weaponry. The mayors of Hiroshima and Nagasaki presented their graphic accounts, as did Lijon Eknilang, a councillor of Rongalap Atoll in the Marshall

Islands, who testified about the reproductive abnormalities common among her people as a result of the radiation fallout from a 1954 nuclear test at Bikini Atoll. The impact of this huge detonation on human health and the environment has stretched over several decades and thousands of miles from ground zero. With the exception of China, the major nuclear powers — the United States, Britain, France, and Russia — along with NATO ally Germany, testified to deny that the Court had jurisdiction to render an opinion and to justify the possession of nuclear weapons for deterrence or self-defence.

All the conflicting testimony from both sides illuminated the chasm between opponents and proponents of nuclear weapons.

New Zealand and Zimbabwe argued strongly against nuclear weapons. New Zealand, seeking to persuade the Court that the principles of humanitarian law forbid their use, or the threat of their use, in any circumstances, argued that under humanitarian law:

- states' choice of weapons of warfare is not unlimited: moreover, states are not free to choose a given weapon simply because it is not specifically prohibited;

- in warfare, states must distinguish between civilians and military objectives, and attacks must be directed solely against military ones. Injury to civilians (collateral damage) must not be excessive in relation to military advantage;

- states must not use weapons that cause superfluous injury or unnecessary suffering;

- The idea of an ongoing obligation to future generations is increasingly recognized in environmental law. States must not use weapons that may be expected to cause widespread, long-term, and severe damage to the natural environment;

- the Geneva Convention and other aspects of customary international law prohibit the use of asphyxiating, poisonous, or other gases. Given the radiation effects of nuclear weapons, this body of law should apply also to nuclear weapons;

- neutral states have the right to be free from harm and injury arising from an armed conflict in which they are not involved.

Zimbabwe lambasted the United States, Russia, Britain, and France for adamantly maintaining their first-use and retaliatory policies on nuclear weapons and then arguing that an opinion from the Court would prevent progress on disarmament negotiations, which the nuclear powers are themselves disrupting. It is "absurd" to claim, as France did in court, that the only role of WHO is "downstream," that it has no competence except after the event. "Does this State believe that WHO should not have conducted its preventive health programs to combat tuberculosis and smallpox?" Zimbabwe rejected outright the nuclear states' claim that modern nuclear weapons are capable of precise targeting and can therefore be directed against specific military objectives without indiscriminate effect on civilians.

The United Kingdom countered by arguing that, inasmuch as the international community is divided over the issue of the legality of nuclear weapons, the Court should not remove the "veil of constructive silence over that sterile debate." To do so would risk making progress on "practical matters." The concept of deterrence is fundamental to the maintenance of the peace and security of a substantial number of states: "We might wish nuclear weapons away, as we might wish away all weapons and, indeed, the whole concept of war and coercion. But nuclear weapons do exist and the Court — as a court of law — must operate not in some idealized world but in the real world." It would be "profoundly destabilizing" to call into question the legal basis of the system of deterrence. The British denied that the use of a nuclear weapon against a military objective would inevitably cause disproportional civilian casualties. A "balance" had to be struck between military damage and civilian casualties. It is an "inescapable feature" of this principle that the greater the military advantage, the greater the civilian risk: "Where what is at stake is the difference between national survival and subjection to conquest which may be of the most brutal and enslaving character, it is dangerously wrong to say that the use of a nuclear weapon could never meet the criterion of proportionality."

The United States argued that the policy of nuclear deterrence has saved many millions of lives from the scourge of war during the past half century. The assumption that any use of nuclear weapons would inevitably escalate into a massive strategic nuclear exchange is unwarranted. The American deterrence strategy is designed to provide a range of options in response to armed aggression, and it will control escalation and terminate armed conflict as soon as possible. The argument that nuclear weapons are inherently indiscriminate is wrong: modern delivery systems are capable of a precise strike. And, the assertion that civilian injury would be excessive in relation to military advantage is speculative: "Whether the use of nuclear weapons in any given instance would result in the infliction of disproportionate collateral destruction or incidental injury to civilians cannot be judged in the abstract."

On July 8, 1996, the Court handed down its 34-page Advisory Opinion. It declined to answer the WHO question on the grounds that the agency, which specializes in health issues, is not competent to put its question to the Court. The second question, submitted by the U.N., evoked a complex answer that cannot be reduced to headline simplicity.

The Court begins by noting the unique characteristics of nuclear weapons, particularly their capacity to cause untold human suffering and their ability to cause damage for generations to come. While the U.N. Charter prohibits the use of force, it also permits self-defence and authorizes military enforcement measures. There is no treaty prohibiting nuclear weapons, as there is for biological and chemical weapons. Certain treaties, covering specific zones of the earth, may be seen as a portent of a future general prohibition, but the international community is profoundly divided on the subject.

The Court reaffirmed the cardinal principles of humanitarian law, which are the following: in order to protect the civilian population, states must never use weapons that are incapable of distinguishing between civilian and military targets; it is prohibited to cause unnecessary suffering to combatants, and hence states do not have unlimited freedom of choice of weapons. Even though nuclear weapons were invented after the established principles and rules of humanitarian law had come into existence, it cannot be concluded that humanitarian law does not apply to them.

The Court then addressed the opposing views: one side holds that recourse to nuclear weapons, regulated by the law of armed conflict, is not prohibited: the other holds that, in view of the necessarily indiscriminate consequences of their use, nuclear weapons can never be compatible with humanitarian law and are therefore prohibited. The Court held that the use of such weapons seems "scarcely reconcilable" with respect for humanitarian law, but added that it could not conclude with certainty that their use would contravene international law in every circumstance. The Court recognized the reality of the strategy of nuclear deterrence, "to which an appreciable section of the international community has adhered for many years." Accordingly, in view of the present state of international law viewed as a whole, the Court "could not reach a definitive conclusion as to the legality or illegality of the use of nuclear weapons by a State in an extreme circumstance of self-defence, in which its very survival would be at stake." However, international stability suffers from these divergent views, and it is important to put an end to this state of affairs: long-promised nuclear disarmament is the most appropriate means of achieving that result. Calling attention to Article VI of the NPT, the Court said that nations are obliged "to achieve a precise result — nuclear disarmament in all its aspects." Nations must pursue negotiations in good faith: "Any realistic search for general and complete disarmament, especially nuclear disarmament, necessitates the cooperation of all States."

Within the Court, two elements were put into one key vote. One paragraph stated: "The threat or use of nuclear weapons would generally be contrary to the rules of international law applicable in armed conflict, and in particular the principles and rules of humanitarian law." The next paragraph said, "The Court cannot conclude definitively whether the threat or use of nuclear weapons would be lawful or unlawful in an extreme circumstance of self-defence, in which the very survival of a State would be at stake." The vote was tied 7-7, but the proposition carried because of the President's tie-breaking power.

In effect, the Court de-legitimized nuclear weapons as a war-fighting strategy, but left open the question of their use in "an extreme circumstance of self-defence."

This "escape hatch" was just what the nuclear states needed to bolster their claim that nuclear weapons are just for defence and, accordingly, the Court's Advisory Opinion would not alter their nuclear deterrence policies. But the 200 pages of the judges' separate opinions gave a sharper edge to the Court's presumed ambivalence. Three of the judges, Weeramantry of Sri Lanka, Koroma of Sierre Leone, and Shahabuddeen of Guyana, all of whom had voted no in the key vote, declared in their statements that the use or threat of use of nuclear weapons is illegal any time, any place. In other words, the passage was not strong enough for them. The seven who voted yes, Bedjaoui of Algeria, Ranjeva of Madagascar, Herczegh of Hungary, Shi of China, Fleischhauer of Germany, Vereshchetin of Russia, and Ferrari Bravo of Italy, said that nuclear weapons would "generally" be contrary to the laws of war. These seven were not so sure whether their use would be lawful in an extreme circumstance of self-defence in which the very survival of a state was at stake. Four other judges, Schwebel of the United States, Oda of Japan, Guillaume of France, and Higgins of the United Kingdom, disagreed with both the propositions and held that no general rule is possible, each case being decided on its own merits. Thus, a total of ten of the fourteen judges took the position either that nuclear weapons could never be lawfully used or that they might be used only in the most exceptional of circumstances.

Lost in the debate over what the numbers really added up to were two other votes in which the Court voted unanimously. In the first, it ruled that any threat or use of nuclear weapons should be compatible with humanitarian law and with specific nuclear weapons treaties. In the second, the whole Court maintained that:

> There exists an obligation to pursue in good faith and bring
> to a conclusion negotiations leading to nuclear disarmament
> in all its aspects under strict and effective international con-
> trol.

Anticipating that the Court's inability to give an unqualified condemnation of nuclear weapons would be perceived as acquiescing with the nuclear states to maintain the status quo, President Bedjaoui, in a separate statement, said that the fact that the Court was unable to go any further should not "in any way be interpreted as leaving the way open to the recognition of the lawfulness of the threat or use of nuclear weapons." He then gave a stinging indictment of nuclear weapons:

> The very nature of this blind weapon... has a destabilizing
> effect on humanitarian law which regulates discernment in
> the type of weapon used. Nuclear weapons, the ultimate evil,
> destabilize humanitarian law which is the law of the lesser
> evil. The existence of nuclear weapons is therefore a chal-
> lenge to the very existence of humanitarian law, not to men-
> tion their long-term effects of damage to the human
> environment, in respect to which the right to life can be
> exercised.

President Bedjaoui added that even if it uses a nuclear weapon only in defence of its very survival, a state cannot exonerate itself from compliance with the "intransgressible" norms of international and humanitarian law. It would be very rash to accord a higher priority to the survival of a State than to the survival of humanity itself.

The absence of a clear and comprehensive law on nuclear weapons was deplored by several judges. Judge Vereshchetin of Russia said the Court cannot be blamed for indecisiveness where the law is itself inconclusive. Judge Guillaume of France held that, inasmuch as the law provides no guidance, states, in the exercise of their sovereignty, remain free to act as they think fit. Contrary to Judge Bedjaoui, he maintains that, in recognizing the question of the survival of a state, the Court has recognized the legality of policies of deterrence. Continuing this theme, Judge Fleischhauer of Germany says that if attacked with nuclear, bacteriological, or chemical weapons threatening its existence, a State could retaliate with nuclear weapons. But that is not the view of Judge Weeramantry. His 88-page dissent deals convincingly with every last argument advanced by the NWS in support of their position, including deterrence, reprisals, internal wars, the doctrine of necessity, and the health hazards of all, including so-called "mini," nuclear weapons. Judge Koroma rejected outright the Court's contention that the current state of the law did not permit the Court to go further. The law exists in substantial and ample form to permit the Court to outlaw nuclear weapons. After analyzing the evidence, Judge Koroma of Sierre Leone came to the conclusion that nuclear weapons are unlawful in all circumstances:

> [Nuclear weapons] are incapable of distinguishing between civilians and military personnel, would result in the death of thousands if not millions of civilians, cause superfluous injury and unnecessary suffering to survivors, affect future generations, damage hospitals and contaminate the natural environment, food and drinking water, with radioactivity, thereby depriving survivors of the means of survival contrary to the Geneva Conventions of 1949 and the 1977 Additional Protocol I thereto.

The Court's Long-range Effect

What is the effect of the World Court Advisory Opinion? At first it might seem minimal. The nuclear states are ignoring it. NATO is hostile to it. The media have generally marginalized it. Nonetheless, the purpose of seeking the World Court's opinion was to take away the moral high ground claimed by nuclear proponents, and in this it was successful. Even a unanimous opinion that the threat or use of nuclear weapons is illegal under any circumstances would not have magically waved away existing stockpiles. The Court seemed well aware of its limited authority in a world not yet ready to accept the enforceability of its decisions. Governments themselves must negotiate nuclear disarmament: it cannot be imposed.

The opinion is a watershed because, for the first time, there is a legal basis for political action to ban nuclear weapons. It is the highest-level legal push ever given to governments to get on with nuclear disarmament. It goes beyond the NPT's Article VI, which obliges nations merely to *pursue* negotiations on nuclear disarmament: the Court has deemed that such negotiations must be *concluded*. Moreover, it explicitly separated the two themes in Article VI: nuclear disarmament, and general and complete disarmament. No longer can the nuclear powers credibly state that nuclear disarmament can only come in the context of general disarmament. The "ultimate evil" must be eliminated urgently.

When the Comprehensive Test Ban Treaty was adopted in 1996, its Preamble stated that the parties to it are "convinced that the present international situation provides an opportunity to take further effective measures towards nuclear disarmament." The Court has underscored this opportunity.

By highlighting the need for *successful* nuclear disarmament, the Court points squarely to the need for a nuclear weapons convention that would prohibit the possession, development, threat, and use of nuclear weapons. The Court's opinion enables politicians and activists who support nuclear disarmament to take the legal high road against nuclear retentionists, who are now vulnerable to accusations of flouting international law. Governments and military leaders will come under pressure to review the legal position of personnel involved in the deployment of nuclear weapons. At the very least, the Court's opinion challenges NATO's doctrine of nuclear deterrence. The Court noted that those who advocate the legality of the use of "clean," low-yield, tactical nuclear weapons had not stated the precise circumstances that might justify their use, "nor whether such limited use would not tend to escalate into the all-out use of high-yield nuclear weapons." The onus is now on NATO's Nuclear Planning Group to demonstrate that its nuclear plans fit the Court's criteria of "extreme" circumstance and would not violate the humanitarian laws of warfare. (In the wake of the Court's opinion, a German court has found that, with the end of the East-West confrontation, there is no "extreme" circumstance that can justify the continuing deployment of nuclear weapons in Europe.)

In its unprecedented acceptance of citizens' Declarations of Conscience, the Court acknowledged the cumulative impact of anti-nuclear efforts in global civil society. The nuclear states are still in a commanding position, but the legal — and public — challenges against their policies have never been so strong.

5

The Movement to
Nuclear Zero

There can be no doubt that a historic momentum is building for the
abolition of nuclear weapons. A month after the World Court handed
down its Advisory Opinion, a group of twenty-eight nations* tabled
in the Conference on Disarmament a three-phase Program of Action
for the complete elimination of nuclear weapons by the year 2020.

The Court's Advisory Opinion is the centrepiece of a growing
movement of politicians, academics, retired military officers, religious leaders, physicians, lawyers, scientists, and community activists
dedicated to the abolition of nuclear weapons. The emergence in civil
society of a movement of organizations determined to advance human security in this way is one of the key aspects of the post-Cold
War era. There are many examples.*

In 1995, the (then) Labour government of Australia established
the Canberra Commission, a group of seventeen distinguished world
figures, to develop ideas and proposals for a concrete and realistic
program to achieve a world totally free of nuclear weapons. Among
the Commissioners: General Lee Butler, former Commander-in-
Chief of the U.S. Strategic Air Command (1991-92) and the U.S.
Strategic Command (1992-94) who was responsible for all the nuclear forces of the American Air Force and Navy; Field Marshall
Lord Carver, former Chief of the British Defence Staff (1973-76);
Robert McNamara, former American Secretary of Defense under
Presidents Kennedy and Johnson; and Joseph Rotblat, President of
the Pugwash Conferences on Science and World Affairs, who won

---

* The twenty-eight were: Algeria, Bangladesh, Brazil, Cameroon, Colombia,
Cuba, DPR Korea, Egypt, Ethiopia, India, Indonesia, Iraq, Iran, Kenya,
Mexico, Mongolia, Morocco, Myanmar, Nigeria, Pakistan, Peru, Senegal, Sri
Lanka, Syria, Venezuela, Vietnam, Zaire, and Zimbabwe.

the 1995 Nobel Peace Prize for his work on nuclear disarmament. The Canberra Commission's report stated that, "Nuclear weapons pose an intolerable threat to all humanity and its habitat," and urged the nuclear states to immediately and "unequivocally" commit themselves to eliminating nuclear weapons, as "Such a commitment would propel the process in the most direct and imaginative way." While getting to zero is the goal, the Commission pointed to a number of practical steps that should be taken immediately, such as taking nuclear forces off alert and removing warheads from delivery vehicles. The report continued:

> The maintenance of a nuclear-weapon-free-world will require an enduring legal framework, linked to the Charter of the United Nations, possibly in the form of a convention on nuclear weapons.

General Butler, who was closely involved in the development of American nuclear doctrine, later said that it was the recognition of "the apocalyptic threat of nuclear weapons" that led him to become a leading figure of the abolition movement. He said that he was led to his new convictions by these concerns:

- a growing alarm that despite all the evidence, the West has yet to fully grasp the monstrous effects of these weapons, that the consequences of their use defy reason, transcend time and space, poison the earth, and deform its inhabitants;

- a deepening dismay at the prolongation of Cold-War policies and practices in a world where national security interests have been utterly transformed;

- that foremost among these policies, deterrence reigns unchallenged, with its embedded assumption of hostility and its preference for forces on high states of alert;

- an acute unease over renewed assertions of the utility of nuclear weapons, especially as a response to chemical or biological attack;

- grave doubt that the present, highly discriminatory regime of nuclear and non-nuclear states can long endure without a credible commitment by the nuclear powers to eliminate their arsenals;

- the horrific prospect of a world seething with enmities, armed to the teeth with nuclear weapons, and hostage to maniacal leaders strongly disposed toward their use.

The Canberra Commission finished its work in the summer of 1996. A few months later, General Butler wrote elsewhere:

> I regret to have to say that the harsh truth is that six years after the end of the Cold War we are still enmeshed in the apocalyptic vocabulary of mutual assured destruction, still in the thrall of the nuclear era. Even worse, strategists persist in conjuring up worlds which spiral toward chaos, and concocting threats which they assert can only be discouraged or expunged by the existence or employment of nuclear weapons.

The Build-up of Informed Opinion

General Butler is far from alone. A group of sixty-one former generals and admirals from seventeen countries*, including the United States and Russia, declared in December, 1996 that "long-term international nuclear policy must be based on the declared principle of continuous, complete and irrevocable elimination of nuclear weapons." They continued:

> We, military professionals, who have devoted our lives to the national security of our countries and our peoples, are convinced that the continuing existence of nuclear weapons in the armories of nuclear powers, and the ever present threat of acquisition of these weapons by others, constitute a peril to global peace and security and to the safety and survival of the people we are dedicated to protect.

This was followed early in 1997 by the preparation of a "Statement by International Civilian Leaders," calling on the nuclear states to "declare unambiguously that their goal is ultimate abolition":

---

* A Canadian, former General Leonard Johnson, Commandant, National Defence College, was one of the sixty-one.

The world is not condemned to live forever with threats of nuclear conflict, or the anxious, fragile peace imposed by nuclear deterrence. Such threats are intolerable and such a peace unworthy. The sheer destructiveness of nuclear weapons invokes a moral imperative for their elimination. That is our mandate. Let us begin.

The Statement, tentatively slated to be released in late 1997, has already been signed by a wide range of former prime ministers, foreign ministers, and ambassadors, including Pierre Trudeau, former Prime Minister of Canada, Malcolm Fraser, former Prime Minister of Australia, Oscar Arias, former President of Costa Rica, Helmut Schmidt, former Chancellor of Germany, Miguel de la Madrid, former President of Mexico, and Ingvar Carlsson, former Prime Minister of Sweden. (As Canada's former Ambassador for Disarmament, I also signed the statement.)

Noting the World Court's opinion, the Canberra Report, and other statements, the European Parliament passed a resolution calling on all European Community members to immediately begin negotiations leading to the conclusion of a convention for the abolition of nuclear weapons. In the United States, serious work is proceeding to convince the Administration and Congress that national security is best served by a nuclear-weapon-free world. The prestigious Henry L. Stimson Center has urged President Clinton to develop a responsible plan to achieve elimination and to begin official study of the problems that will have to be overcome to secure a world without nuclear weapons. An international group of fifty scientists and engineers has published technical documents outlining the steps required to get to nuclear zero. The Pugwash Movement, made up of physical and social scientists from around the world, recently published a book *A Nuclear-Weapon-Free World: Desirable? Feasible?* examining all the problems of verification and safeguarding.

This specialized work is backed by Abolition 2000, an international citizens' movement working to conclude by 2000 negotiations on a treaty to eliminate nuclear weapons in stages, within a time-bound framework, with provisions for effective verification and enforcement. The Abolition 2000 Statement, calling upon all states to enter such negotiations immediately, has been endorsed by some 700 organizations on six continents.

All this activity is greatly adding to the strength of the public case against nuclear weapons. A nuclear-weapon-free world is no longer

a fanciful notion, but is increasingly recognized as the central item
on the global security agenda. It is not only desirable, but feasible,
and can be achieved in a step-by-step manner — once the goal is
firmly set. Lack of political will by the nuclear states is the only true
barrier.

Arguments Against Nuclear Weapons

From a strategic viewpoint, the case for the elimination of nuclear
weapons is based on these major arguments: the uselessness of nuclear weapons, the risk of accident and terrorism, and the repercussions of the disparity among nuclear haves and have-nots.

Nuclear weapons are either powerless to address, or in some cases
simply exacerbate, the most prevalent threats to national security in
today's world, including terrorism, ethnic conflicts, state disintegration, humanitarian disasters, and economic crises. The destructiveness of nuclear weapons is so great that they have no military utility
against a comparably equipped opponent. Their possible acquisition
by terrorist groups is, of course, a growing threat to the international
community. Yet, the very fact that some nations are permitted to
stockpile nuclear weapons is a stimulus for proliferation, and only
hastens the day terrorism may go nuclear.

The possession of nuclear weapons by some states stimulates
others to acquire them, reducing security for all. It is untenable for
the five permanent, veto-wielding members of the Security Council
to maintain nuclear weapons, even at reduced levels, while proscribing their acquisition by all other countries. Even a permanent condition of minimum deterrence is not desirable because, sooner or later,
other states will seek the power and status conferred by nuclear
weapons. Why should nuclear weapons be necessary for American
security, but not for the security of Israel, or India, or Pakistan?
Indeed, the smaller states might argue that they have a greater need
for the equalizing power of nuclear warheads. The argument that
nuclear weapons should be retained because they deter conventional
wars is false. Conventional wars persist, despite the possession of
nuclear weapons by nuclear states involved in them. And, if they
really did deter conventional war, it would only act as an incentive
for virtually every country to acquire its own nuclear weapons. Proliferation would run amuck.

The argument that nuclear weapons cannot be dis-invented ("the
genie cannot be put back in the bottle") is belied by present treaties

banning the production of chemical and biological weapons, which also cannot be "dis-invented." The "bottle" can indeed be contained, by stringent verification to confirm the destruction of current stockpiles and to control the means of production. Such a verification regime is technically possible and would become politically viable in a world that was already partially demilitarized through minimum deterrence, advances in conventional disarmament, and international barriers to the arms trade. A reduction in the number of authoritarian regimes through the spread of democracy would also be a new global security anchor.

While the strategic arguments against nuclear weapons are compelling in their own right, I do not believe they will by themselves convince the nuclear powers to make an unequivocal commitment to abolition. Rather, we must concentrate on the pre-eminent fact that nuclear weapons contravene humanitarian law, which has been accepted through the centuries as the only basis for civilization's survival. Here the legal and moral arguments against nuclear weapons intertwine with the strategic: since nuclear weapons can destroy all life on the planet, they imperil all humanity ever stood for, and humanity itself. During the acrimonious years of the Cold War, when the emphasis on the military doctrine of nuclear deterrence was used as a constant justification for the nuclear build-up, the public seemed blind to the horror of nuclear weapons. But now, in the post-Cold War era characterized by East-West partnership, there is no excuse for shielding ourselves from the assault on life itself that nuclear weapons represent.

The force of the movement for the abolition of nuclear weapons, although gathering considerable strength, is rebuffed by the Western nuclear states, which are still in a dominant position. That is where we are today. The nuclear powers will not give up their weapons without assurance that a nuclear-free global security system is viable. The "threshold" states will not give up their nuclear options, and the leading members of the non-aligned movement will not stop their criticism of the nuclear states without seeing proof of a commitment to move to nuclear zero on a specified timetable. The START III talks, in which the Americans and Russians plan deeper cuts, are an important step forward, but without drawing the British, French, and Chinese into negotiations where the stated goal is to get to zero over the next two decades or so, the present impasse will remain. Those nations without nuclear weapons would instantly support an unequivocal commitment by the nuclear powers because it would give

new coherence to the entire spectrum of non-proliferation, disarmament, and arms-limitation efforts currently being pursued at global
and regional levels.

In order to generate confidence within the international community that the nuclear states are sincere about nuclear de-escalation,
even if not yet willing to make an iron-clad commitment to zero, the
abolition movement is pushing them to take certain immediate, interim steps. These would significantly reduce the risk of nuclear war,
and so enhance global security.

Taking nuclear forces off alert is at the top of the interim list. The
continuing practice of maintaining nuclear missiles on alert, whether
on land-based or sea-based vehicles, needlessly sustains a high risk
of hair-trigger accident or misjudgement. It sends the unmistakable
message that nuclear weapons serve a vital security role, and this is
entirely inappropriate to the post-Cold War era. Russia and the
United States maintain they are no longer "targeting" each other's
cities: but this is only a symbolic gesture, and is reversible in a matter
of minutes. Taking missiles out of operational mode, while not a
substitute for disarmament, would build confidence in the disarmament process.

While of signal importance, the existing START agreements do
not require that withdrawn warheads be disassembled and destroyed.
Nor do the they address the matter of the disposition of fissile
material in warheads removed from deployment. This material represents the core element of nuclear weapons, and it should be completely removed from weapons sites. The physical separation of
warheads from delivery vehicles would reinforce the gains achieved
by taking nuclear forces off alert. A START III agreement should
require the verified dismantling of redundant warheads. Nuclear warheads removed from strategic and tactical missiles should be stored
in national repositories under international inspection. A range of
intrusive verification procedures that have already been accepted by
the United States and Russia, with the implementation of the Intermediate Nuclear Forces Treaty, could be the basis of a verification
regime to ensure that no state would gain a meaningful advantage by
its ability to re-assemble its nuclear force for first-strike capability.

In 1991, the United States and the Soviet Union pledged to remove
all non-strategic (that is, short-range or "tactical") nuclear weapons
from ships and submarines and store them ashore. The nuclear states
should follow this up by removing all tactical nuclear weapons from
the sites where they are deployed. American tactical nuclear weapons

deployed in Western Europe serve no security purpose. To the contrary, they send a message that Moscow is still not to be trusted, thus feeding fears in Russia that NATO harbours aggressive designs against it.

The political climate would also be improved by a joint commitment by the nuclear powers not to be the first to use, or threaten to use, nuclear weapons. Only China has made such a commitment, while NATO has always resisted it on the grounds that nuclear weapons may be needed to thwart a conventional attack. The World Court decision has removed any legitimacy NATO's stand may have had.

Such interim steps by the nuclear states need to be reinforced by action to prevent further horizontal proliferation. Proliferation pressures in South Asia, the Middle East, and the Korean Peninsula could prejudice prospects for eliminating nuclear weapons. That is why the spread of nuclear-weapon-free zones is vital. Already, most of the southern hemisphere is free of nuclear weapons. Other nuclear-free zones should now be established in South Asia, in Central Europe, and from the Black Sea to the Baltic.

It must become an internationally accepted norm to build a nuclear-weapon-free world. National arguments that nuclear weapons are needed because others have them would then not apply. Successive steps toward nuclear disarmament would build confidence that zero can be reached. But separate steps alone do not provide a program with a definable goal. A single legal instrument specifying abolition as the goal is needed. That instrument is a Nuclear Weapons Convention.

6

The Outline of an Abolition Plan

Would you live in a house where your neighbours on either side filled their homes with explosives and arsenals aimed at each other and were ready to fire at a moment's notice? Local law protects you from such a threat. Yet on a global level, technology has produced this very situation.

Through five decades, the United Nations has been hamstrung by the absence of effective world law in its efforts to achieve the peaceful resolution of conflicts. Neither ethical values nor political strategies can guarantee peace and security. Rather, a system of law is required. This is not a utopian dream, but the hard reality of a modern world whose interdependent features make us all, irrespective of geography, vulnerable to one another. Just as nobody would expect to live in a community without the protection of the rule of law, so everyone's security and safety today demands a body of enforceable world law. The system of world law we have today is rudimentary. In the face of the need for legislative, executive, and judicial institutions to maintain world order, our present international organizations are alarmingly weak.

Every orderly society is based on three foundations: laws to define minimum standards of behaviour; courts to determine whether agreed laws have been violated, and a system of effective law enforcement. In the international arena, the three conditions exist only in an elementary way. It is true that the U.N. is quietly building up a body of law that will — when the political will develops — be the basis for world institutions with some teeth in them. More than 300 international treaties, on topics as varied as human rights conventions and agreements on the use of outer space, have been enacted through the efforts of the U.N. Nonetheless, there are very few "laws" that are universally respected, World Court rulings are not necessarily binding, and enforcement measures against non-compliant states are honoured more in the breach than in observance.

In 1982, former U.N. Secretary-General Javier Perez de Cuellar, alarmed at the Cold War arms build-up, condemned governments for ignoring their own signatures on the U.N. Charter. "We are perilously near to a new international anarchy," he lamented. Two years later, pointing squarely at the two superpowers, he asked, "By what right do they decide the fate of all humanity?" The Soviet Union's choke-hold over Eastern Europe was a blatant flouting of international law, but after Mikhail Gorbachev's arrival, the country made a U-turn in foreign policy. At the United Nations, Gorbachev renounced the use or threat of force as an instrument of foreign policy: "This applies above all to nuclear arms." He advanced a range of proposals to guarantee a secure world, a central concept of which was a "system of universal law and order." The jurisdiction of the World Court in human rights cases, he said, "must be binding on all states."

In the mid-1980s, Nicaragua took the United States to the World Court over the issue of American mining of Nicaraguan harbours. Three days before Nicaragua filed its complaint, Washington gave notice that, effective immediately, it would not consider the Court's jurisdiction compulsory, notwithstanding a 1946 declaration by the United States accepting the compulsory jurisdiction of the Court. The United States then withdrew from participation in the Court's proceedings. In the end, the Court ruled against the Americans, finding that the mining, the arming of the Contras, and attacks on oil installations were contrary to "general principles of humanitarian law." Citing this and other examples, Senator David Patrick Moynihan of New York observed: "There is clear evidence that the United States is moving away from its long-established concern for and advocacy of international legal norms of State behaviour."

As the only superpower left, and as the centrepiece of NATO, the American attitude toward the development of international law in the post-Cold War era is crucial. The American attitude to international law appears to be that it is optional, at best. When it needed a Security Council resolution to legitimize the Gulf War in 1991, it generated support through the United Nations, but it ignored the U.N. by invading Panama. It attacked the viability of the Anti-Ballistic Missile Treaty by advancing the concept of the Strategic Defence Initiative ("Star Wars"). It refuses to join in any international guarantee to keep weapons out of space. New questions are now bursting onto

a turbulent international scene: human rights as international obligations; environmental concerns that obliterate boundaries; the elimination of nuclear weapons. The United States, frustrated by the
behaviour of others in a world of rising nationalisms and dynamic
globalism, must be helped, especially by its friends, to recognize that
the only hope for peace in the next century is to replace the law of
force with the force of law.

Great questions of law are sweeping in from the horizon. A permanent International Criminal Court, now in preparation, will likely
come into existence by 2000. It promises to bring those who commit
crimes under international law before the bar of justice. Currently,
there is no such jurisdiction, except as it has been exercised on an
ad hoc basis in international tribunals for the former Yugoslavia and
Rwanda. The new court will likely include among its crimes genocide, crimes against humanity, and war crimes. At a preparatory
meeting, Syria proposed including nuclear weapons in a list of crimes
against humanity because of the asphyxiating and poisonous characteristics of the gases they can unleash. The nuclear states undoubtedly will not endorse any court that could hold their leaders
accountable for the threat or use of nuclear weapons in all circumstances. But what of the future? Could we not look forward to the
day when an established International Criminal Court would include
nuclear weapons under the definition of genocide, crimes against
humanity, or war crimes?

Political Development of New Law

This returns the question, as the World Court itself did, to the political arena. The only way to get a viable international law banning
nuclear weapons, and hence making it an international crime to use
them, is to advance the political process to greater maturity. This
cannot be done by coercion, but the nuclear states are not immune
from the court of world opinion. That court is only now emerging
into a powerful force.

The World Court opinion, the Canberra Report, the statement by
the generals and admirals, and other informed viewpoints are having
a profound effect on the search for a legal instrument that the international community can agree on to ban nuclear weapons. There are
a number of legal options available. For example, the NPT could be
amended to transform it into a treaty banning nuclear weapons, or
an entirely new treaty could be negotiated. If the latter, where would

the negotiations take place? In the General Assembly? In the Conference on Disarmament (which operates by consensus)? In a new forum? Should a total ban on nuclear weapons emerge as the end product of a series of unrelated steps, or should it be the declared goal of a set of comprehensive negotiations? Should a fixed timetable be set for the negotiations? Should they proceed at their own pace, subject to the rise and fall of political actors? While none of these questions is yet answered, at least to the degree that there is general political acceptance of the answer, there is gathering support for a Nuclear Weapons Convention (NWC) as a single legal instrument that would entail a binding commitment to the elimination of nuclear weapons.

In 1996, the American-based Lawyers' Committee on Nuclear Policy established a committee of lawyers, scientists, disarmament experts, and diplomats to draft a NWC that would prohibit the development, production, testing, stockpiling, transfer, use, and threat of use of nuclear weapons, and provide for their elimination. Such a comprehensive treaty would be clearly focussed on the elimination of nuclear weapons, whereas many of the existing and prospective steps have arms control rather than disarmament as their basis.

A comprehensive approach would include step-by-step negotiations on coordinated phases as part of the process leading to elimination. Relying only on step-by-step negotiations, with no overall plan, would offer no guarantee that a final goal would ever be reached. It is doubtful whether existing global treaties banning biological and chemical weapons could ever have been reached only through incremental steps. In fact, the achievement of minor steps can actually delay progress toward the ultimate goal of elimination. The Partial Test Ban Treaty of 1963 did not end nuclear tests, it merely shifted them from the atmosphere (a blessing in itself, of course) to underground.

A comprehensive approach would keep negotiations going past each marker, thus maintaining the momentum to complete the process. Accordingly, the international community could see where it was headed, the attainment of interim goals could be measured, and the non-nuclear states could be assured that the international community was truly on its way to ending the odious two-class system of nuclear haves and have-nots. Several states have resisted accepting partial steps without an agreed framework for elimination. This is why India has refused to sign the CTBT. Moreover, a comprehensive, non-discriminatory approach would include the threshold states and the potential nuclear weapon states, thus eliminating the continuing risk of nuclear proliferation. This latter point should be particularly appealing to the nuclear powers.

The 59-page model presented by the Lawyers' Committee on Nuclear Policy, drawing on the technical language of other conventions, such as the one covering chemical weapons, demonstrates the feasibility of a comprehensive plan and is intended to stimulate governments to start negotiations. The model addresses concerns regarding verification, phases of implementation, prevention of clandestine production or acquisition, security in a non-nuclear environment, and possible non-compliance.

The Preamble to the model begins:

> Convinced that the existence of nuclear weapons poses a threat to all humanity and that their use would have catastrophic consequences for all the creatures of this Earth;
>
> Noting that the destructive effects of nuclear weapons upon life on earth are uncontrollable whether in time or space;
>
> Aware that amongst weapons of mass destruction, the abolition of which is recognized as being in the collective security interest of all people and States, nuclear weapons are unprecedented and unequalled in destructive potential;
>
> Affirming that the inherent dignity and equal and inalienable rights of all members of the human family include the right to life, liberty, peace and the security of person;
>
> Convinced that all countries have an obligation to make every effort to achieve the goal of eliminating nuclear weapons, the terror which they hold for humankind and the threat which they pose to life on Earth...

Section I indicates the model's scope:

> Each State Party to this Convention undertakes never under any circumstances:
>
> a. to use or threaten to use nuclear weapons;
>
> b. to engage in any military or other preparations to use nuclear weapons;

c. to research, develop, test, produce, otherwise acquire, deploy, stockpile, maintain, retain, or transfer nuclear weapons;

d. to research, develop, test, produce, otherwise acquire, stockpile, retain, transfer or use special nuclear materials;

e. to research, develop, test, produce, otherwise acquire, deploy, stockpile, maintain, retain, or transfer delivery vehicles for the purpose of delivering nuclear weapons;

f. to research, develop, test, produce, otherwise acquire, stockpile, maintain, retain, or transfer nuclear weapons components or equipment as specified in this Convention;

g. to assist, encourage, induce or permit, in any way, directly or indirectly, anyone to engage in any activity prohibited under this Convention.

A NWC would not stand by itself. Rather, it would be the anchor of a phased program that would culminate in the complete elimination of existing stockpiles of nuclear weapons. Here is what a phased program could look like:

First Phase

a. negotiation of a convention to prohibit the use or threat of use of nuclear weapons;

b. all nuclear weapons taken off alert status and removed from delivery vehicles;

c. negotiation of a treaty banning the production of fissile material for nuclear weapons;

d. implementation of the START II Treaty and negotiations on START III for further Russian and American reductions.

Second Phase

a. reductions in British, French, and Chinese stockpiles;

b. all nuclear weapons production and research facilities closed;

c. progressive and balanced reduction of delivery vehicles;

d. establishment of a single, integrated, multilateral agency to ensure verification and compliance with reduction and closure programs.

Third Phase

a. adoption of principles and mechanisms for a cooperative global security system;

b. all nuclear materials for peaceful purposes put under strict, effective and exclusive international control;

c. all nuclear weapons destroyed under international inspection.

Getting Negotiations Started

How long would it take to implement such a phased program? The short answer is: a long time. Estimates vary between fifteen and twenty-five years. The Western nuclear powers are adamantly opposed to any sort of timetable, even assuming their agreement to move toward the goal. The Abolition 2000 movement wants negotiations on a NWC to be concluded by 2000, but has not specified how long implementation might take. The Canberra Commission wrestled with the question of a timetable, but elected not to specify one in order not to have their report summarily dismissed by the nuclear states. Certainly, a limiting factor to any timetable may be the level of confidence in the verification regime required to take the final step to complete elimination. The Commission diplomatically chose ambiguous language:

The Canberra Commission remains convinced of the basic importance of agreed targets and guidelines which would drive the process inexorably toward the ultimate objective of final elimination, at the earliest possible time.

Some careful diplomatic strategies are called for. The 1995 NPT Extension Conference set 1996 as the target for the achievement of a comprehensive Test Ban Treaty *because there was political will to achieve it*. President John F. Kennedy set the end of the 1960s as the target for putting a man on the moon *because there was political will to achieve it*. Timetables can only be addressed when there is political will on the principle concerned. The Western nuclear states lack the political will for abolition. Therefore, they must be encouraged to accept the growing global wisdom that the security of all states would be improved in a nuclear-weapon-free world. Then, the reasoning behind timetables — so that progress can be measured through the various stages — would become acceptable. The actual year when zero is reached is less important than the "unequivocal" commitment by the nuclear powers *now* to get there. "The earliest possible time" must not become code for "the 22nd century," as "ultimate" has become code for "never." There is no reason — technical or financial — for the world to endure nuclear weapons for more than another 25 years.

Where should negotiations for a NWC take place?

When 46 States, led by Malaysia, followed up the World Court's opinion with a resolution at the General Assembly calling for multi-lateral negotiations on a NWC, they did not specify precisely the locale, but they indirectly suggested the Conference on Disarmament. They also refrained from saying that elimination should be accomplished in a time-bound framework, other than that the negotiations should begin in 1997. Despite this vagueness, the Western nuclear states and Russia still voted against the resolution. (China voted in favour.) It carried, with 115 in favour, 22 against, and 32 abstentions, but it is inoperative without the support of all the nuclear states.

Negotiations among the five nuclear powers alone would not likely be accepted by the non-nuclear states (which would also have to live with the results). It has been suggested that the five take into their negotiations one other state representing the interests of the non-nuclear states. This also would not likely be popularly received. The Conference on Disarmament seems an apt forum because it has already been mandated by the U.N. to deal with nuclear disarmament. Moreover, it was the negotiating forum for the NPT and biological and chemical conventions. But its consensus rule immobilized it when negotiating the CTBT: when India balked, discussion shifted to the General Assembly. A special negotiating body could be struck by the General Assembly, as was done for the negotiations on the Law of the Sea, or the ongoing NPT talks could call for a conference to negotiate a NWC as a means of implementing Article VI of the NPT. However, the threshold states of India, Pakistan, and Israel are not members of the NPT. Would they join it on condition that it become a negotiating forum for a global ban?

The Conference on Disarmament is the most likely place to begin negotiations. It has its own structure and long experience in analyzing disarmament questions. However, the importance of the NPT process in energizing the political will to make the Conference on Disarmament productive should not be lost. Locale is not the main issue. The issue, at its essential level, is the willingness of the Western nuclear states to commit themselves unequivocally to negotiate the elimination of nuclear weapons and to accept a process that drives inexorably to abolition at the earliest possible time. Everything else will fall into place once that commitment is sincerely given.

7

The Role of
Middle Power Countries

In the early 1980s, I learned the value of key countries working together for peace. I was part of a political initiative launched by Parliamentarians for Global Action, a world-wide network of parliamentarians dedicated to advancing disarmament and development issues. (Originally called Parliamentarians for World Order, it has a membership of more than 1,100 parliamentarians in eighty-one countries. I was its first elected International President.) Deeply concerned about the Washington-Moscow stalemate and the escalating nuclear arms race, we decided to visit the leaders of important, middle power countries and encourage them to take a more active, personal role in urging the Big Two to resume nuclear weapons negotiations. Six leaders on five continents responded to us favourably, and out of this exercise emerged the "Six-Nation Initiative." The leaders of Mexico, Argentina, Tanzania, Greece, India, and Sweden signed a Call for Action and met together in New Delhi in 1984 to press the two superpowers to stop nuclear testing and get on with negotiations. The Six-Nation Initiative became an important diplomatic effort because it was an effective channel for the views of many governments, parliaments, and citizens working for common security. The Initiative could not, of course, take sole credit for the resumption of Soviet-American negotiations, which soon did get back on course: there were other factors and events inter-playing on the world stage, but it was an important element in demonstrating world support for nuclear disarmament to the two superpowers.

Our work on the Six-Nation Initiative had been influenced by the 1982 Report of the Independent Commission on Disarmament and Security Issues, headed by Olaf Palme, the late Prime Minister of Sweden. The Palme Report broke ground internationally because it shifted responsibility for world peace from the exclusive preserve of the superpowers and made it the job of other nations as well. All nations, rich and poor, peaceful and bellicose, socialist and capitalist, are bound together by their vulnerability to attack with nuclear, chemical, and biological weapons. The principle of common security that Palme advanced asserted that countries could only find security in cooperation aimed at attaining the limitation, reduction, and eventual abolition of nuclear arms. Palme applied the principle to economic as well as to military security: "Countries are joined together by economic interdependence as well as by the threat of destruction." His report called for a "doctrine of common security" to replace nuclear deterrence. International peace would then rest on a commitment to joint survival, rather than on a threat of mutual destruction.

Over the years, the idea of common security continued to develop. The meaning of security broadened from military protection to human safety in the face of such chronic threats as hunger, disease, and repression, as well as safety from sudden and harmful disruptions in the patterns of daily life. In 1992, a summit meeting of the U.N. Security Council declared that the absence of war and military conflict does not, in itself, ensure international peace and security: "The non-military sources of instability in the economic, social, humanitarian and ecological fields have become threats to peace and security." A series of U.N. global conferences dealing with the integrated agenda for security — environment and development, population, economic and social issues, women's issues — has tried to translate these multiple bases for human security into concrete programs of action. All this work has emphasized that the primary goals of global security policy should be to prevent conflict and war and to maintain the integrity of the planet's life-support systems by eliminating the economic, social, environmental, political, and military conditions that threaten them.

What this mammoth effort of the 1990s has shown is that no single global security problem can be solved in isolation from others, and that no one country can solve problems by itself. The agenda is too big, and there are too many issues and actors involved. A cooperative effort for global security is essential. The comprehensive basis for common security was taken a step further by the Commission on Global Governance, which coined the term "global governance." This Commission was an independent group of twenty-eight international leaders — headed by Prime Minister Ingvar Carlsson of Sweden and Shridath Ramphal, former Secretary-General of the

Commonwealth — which examined ways for the global community to better manage its affairs. The Commission defined "governance" as the sum of the many ways individuals and institutions, public and private, manage their common affairs. Although states are primary actors, they do not bear the whole burden of global governance. Rather, "It is a broad, dynamic, complex process of interactive decision-making that is constantly evolving and responding to changing circumstances." Rejecting the notion that global governance means global government, the Commission insisted that global governance embraces the cooperative efforts of governments *and* citizens' movements, as well as transnational corporations, academia, and the mass media:

> The emergence of a global civil society, with many movements reinforcing the sense of human solidarity, is one of the most positive features of our time. It reflects a large increase in the capacity and will of people to take control of and improve their own lives.

Common security and global governance are joined by a third new element in the post-Cold War era: preventive diplomacy. As defined by Boutros Boutros Ghali, former U.N. Secretary-General, preventive diplomacy is action that prevents disputes from arising between parties, that prevents existing disputes from escalating into conflicts, and that limits the spread of conflicts when they do occur. Preventive diplomacy has long been practiced by the U.N., which has used quiet diplomatic efforts to avert more than 80 imminent wars. But it is only now, with the end of superpower control over the actions of many nations that was a hallmark of the Cold War, that preventive diplomacy has acquired a new status. Boutros Ghali listed it with peace-making, peacekeeping, and peace-building as modern tools in the U.N.'s long search for international peace and security. The most desirable and efficient use of diplomacy is to ease tensions before they result in conflict: fact-finding and early warning are part of this process.

Why a New Coalition Is Needed

The United Nations ought to be the place where common security, global governance, and preventive diplomacy all come together to deal with the nuclear weapons issue. In some ways, this is happening.

The General Assembly resolution calling for negotiations to begin on a NWC is just the tip of the iceberg — over the years, there have been many other efforts by U.N. members to make solid progress on disarmament, and these have crystallized into what is called the "bible" of disarmament, the Final Document of the 1978 U.N. First Special Session on Disarmament. It called for "a comprehensive, phased programme with agreed time-frames, whenever feasible, for progressive and balanced reduction of stockpiles of nuclear weapons and their means of delivery, leading to their ultimate and complete elimination at the earliest possible time." Yet the U.N., hampered by the veto power possessed by each of the five nuclear states, has not been able to implement the declared program.

Since 1978, the U.N. has survived stormy years, and it is still rocked by turbulence today. It won the Nobel Peace Prize in 1988 for its peacekeeping efforts, but has also been roundly criticized by hostile elements for not stopping wars. It works assiduously to promote development for the world's poorest, but is itself nearly bankrupt.

It is not that the U.N. does not know how to build the conditions for peace: rather it is prevented by the rich and powerful from doing what must be done to shore up the pillars of security. The intransigence of the United States Congress in failing to cooperate with the administration to pay the long-overdue American assessments (more than $1 billion) reflects the hostility of right-wing opponents to the global security agenda the U.N. represents. The U.N. has been crippled by the attacks on it. A reform process is underway in a desperate attempt to mollify the most virulent of the critics, but the organization's success over the next few years will be determined by whether or not it merely survives. The success of Kofi Annan, the current Secretary-General selected after Washington vetoed the re-election of Boutros Ghali, will be measured by how well he is able to placate Congress and thus get American money flowing again. Annan's plans for reform call for bold institutional, cultural, and managerial changes to the way the U.N. operates — changes that will certainly help it prepare for the challenges of the next century. But any deep-seated, meaningful reform will require a whole new attitude on the part of the nuclear states. The Security Council must be enlarged to make it more democratic, a permanent peacekeeping force will have to be created, and an adequate funding mechanism must be put in place that will allow the entire U.N. system to function smoothly and efficiently.

It pains me to say this, but I have come to the conclusion that, by itself, the U.N. cannot adequately deal with the new global security agenda, and it is certainly incapable of engineering the abolition of nuclear weapons. It must be helped — not just in ordinary, business-as-usual terms, but through a vigorous, focussed campaign of important middle-power nations with the willpower to assert their right to influence the common security agenda and the stamina not to be deflected or dismissed by the nuclear states. British economist Barbara Ward argued twenty-five years ago that the middle powers *can* lead the way in new experiments of cooperation: "The superpowers are too vast, too unwieldy, too locked in their own responsibilities. The great mass of states are too poor and too shaky. It is the middle powers ... who occupy about the right position on the scale of influence." With the end of the Cold War, the day of the middle powers has arrived. The abolition of nuclear weapons, the central element in the quest for common security, must now be taken up by a new coalition of middle powers. Their preventive diplomacy can save the nuclear states from the folly of their present course.

This coalition must be formed by a departure from the standard U.N. groupings — East, West, non-aligned — born of the Cold War. It must be a coalition of states that wield a certain economic clout, are trusted by the United States, have good records in seeking disarmament, and can get along. I have in mind Canada, Japan, Mexico, Australia, New Zealand, Norway, Sweden, Malaysia, Egypt, and South Africa. There might be others (Ireland, for instance, because it has not been intimidated by the British and French from speaking out in the European Union) but these ten would be enough to form a workable team. In cooperation, they have the capacity to play an unprecedented role for peace.

Japan has the best credentials of any country in the world to speak out for the abolition of nuclear weapons. Mexico, a member of the North American Free Trade Agreement, originated the Treaty of Tlatelolco, which preserves Latin America from nuclear weapons. Australia sponsored the Canberra Commission on the Elimination of Nuclear Weapons. New Zealand, a small country that has stood up to the United States on nuclear issues by banning nuclear-armed and powered ships from its shores, voted for negotiations for a NWC. Norway, like Denmark and Iceland, which are also members of NATO, broke with the NATO line and abstained on the NWC vote. Sweden, a neutral country that has renounced the development of nuclear weapons, has historically given strong leadership on this issue. Malaysia, though still a poor country, sponsored the NWC resolution and is a positive influence in the non-aligned movement. Egypt, as the first Arab country to recognize Israel, is a political heavyweight in the Middle East and commands Washington's respect. South Africa, having built, and then destroyed, six nuclear weapons, has become a strong voice for progressive steps toward nuclear disarmament.

The ten need to work out a joint strategy to put pressure on the nuclear powers to commit themselves "unequivocally" to negotiations for abolition. While all five must be engaged, it is the United States that must be the primary focus. Because of their historical relationships with Washington, each of the ten will be listened to by the American government.

Canada's Special Role

Canada is ideally situated to lead, or at least stimulate, the beginning of this new coalition.

The 1997 U.N. Human Development Report once again named Canada as having the highest standard of living in the world, measured in terms of human development. By a combination of all the indicators — life expectancy, educational attainment, income level — Canada is the choicest place to live of all the 186 countries that make up the U.N. In natural resources of land, minerals, forests, and water, in space, stable population base, industry, and technology, in international reputation, and membership in every important world body, Canada holds a privileged position.

As a diplomat and parliamentarian at the United Nations for many years, I have always been impressed, sometimes overwhelmed, by the confidence other countries place in Canada. They see us as a non-colonial, caring country, closely attached to the United States, but struggling to express our own identity and values. Canada's enthusiastic commitment to peacekeeping (Canada's Lester B. Pearson won the Nobel Peace Prize for originating the concept of U.N. peacekeeping during the 1956 Suez crisis) and its exceptional work in advancing scientific and political steps in verification have won the country renown. Although Canada is thirtieth in population size in the world, the country is the eighth-largest overall supporter of U.N. activities. Its bilingual capacity and, on the whole, progressive immigration policies since World War II have opened up the country to people of many races and cultures, and have enabled the country to project an open, progressive society.

Canada's credentials in nuclear issues are also impressive. As a member of the Manhattan Project, which originated the atomic bomb, Canada was the first country in the world to both have the technical capacity to build nuclear weapons and to renounce that ability. At the 1995 NPT Review and Extension Conference, Canada led the way in garnering the votes necessary to ensure the indefinite extension of the Treaty. At the 1997 preparatory meeting for the 2000 review, Canada explicitly rejected the American contention that getting to nuclear zero depends first on general disarmament: "We do not accept any explicit or implicit linkage, or interpretation of Article VI, that nuclear disarmament will be achieved only when general and complete disarmament has been achieved, or when every last bow and arrow or Swiss army knife is gone."

This is not to say that Canada is on the side of the angels when it comes to nuclear weapons. Though disavowing nuclear weapons of its own, Canada is a member of, and actively supports, the nuclear policies of NATO and NORAD, including the first-use option and the necessity of a missile defence system. Canada provides air space and low-level flight ranges for nuclear bomber training and hosts visits by nuclear-powered and nuclear-armed submarines. As well, it produces and exports components for nuclear weapon delivery vehicles, such as bombers and submarines.

There is actually profound ambiguity in Canadian policy dealing with security questions. Throughout the Cold War, Canada lived behind the American nuclear shield and was thereby able to keep defence expenditures relatively low. Washington made it clear throughout the Cold War that it expected Canada's support on security issues. Canada always voted against nuclear-freeze resolutions at the U.N., because the United States was determined not to put a cap on the development of nuclear weapons. A 1983 peace initiative of Prime Minister Pierre Trudeau was laudable and helped to influence the world climate, but it was derided by American officials.

American antipathy toward the new approaches to common security has constrained what should otherwise have been Canadian promotion of the kind of international security regime that is a natural outgrowth of Canadian values. Those values certainly include the upholding of international law. In a major 1995 foreign policy document, *Canada in the World*, Ottawa solemnly affirmed that:

The rule of law is the essence of civilized behaviour both within and among nations ... Canada will remain in the forefront of those countries working to expand the rule of law internationally.

Canada tried to show its attachment to this sentiment by voting for the paragraph in the NWC resolution that upheld the World Court's Advisory Opinion, but then, under Washington's influence, it voted against both starting negotiations immediately and on the resolution as a whole. Such a split Canadian vote might suffice as an expedient transitional strategy, but it cannot endure with any credibility.

There is no such thing as purism in politics. The fact that Canada's hands are not perfectly clean does not invalidate its potential for taking, in the new post-Cold War environment, decisive steps to further its own and global security. During the Cold War, Canada called for a halt to horizontal nuclear proliferation while allowing vertical proliferation to continue: the rich, technologically developed nations could continue to pile up arms, but the developing countries were proscribed from acquiring them. This discriminating approach to nuclear weapons might once have been tolerated, but it is no longer either acceptable or viable.

The future has caught up with this Canadian ambiguity. Canada can no longer espouse the development of international law and at the same time acquiesce in NATO's outmoded nuclear doctrine. These positions cannot be reconciled: NATO may be powerful, but it is not right. Canada must be in the forefront of those nations calling for a full review of its nuclear weapons policies.

While the Cold War raged, I was prohibited, as Canada's Ambassador for Disarmament, from saying that Canada should declare itself a nuclear-weapon-free zone. The reason, I was told, was that we lived under NATO's nuclear umbrella. That rationale has now evaporated. What is inhibiting Canada today from independent action to rid the world of nuclear weapons? The answer is still the United States. Fear of economic retaliation is a strong motivation not to cross swords with Washington unless it is absolutely necessary.

Without much notice, the Canadian government has set up a Global Issues Bureau to develop policy in the fields of human security and sustainable development. It took, as its first project, an examination of the root causes of human insecurity. Poverty, environmental degradation, crime, and terrorism all spawn violence throughout the world, striking fear into countless millions. The arms trade makes massive violence possible. And the threat of nuclear weapons can carry violence to unheard of levels. But Canadian public opinion for nuclear disarmament is stronger than is generally realized. Bill Graham, M.P., who has served as Chairman of the Foreign Affairs and International Trade Committee, says he had received more mail on the nuclear weapons issue than on any other. But with the media asleep, the public generally is not aroused. It seems that, too often, democracy only acts under the lash of necessity. With courageous political leadership, bureaucratic flexibility, and a push from the public, Canada could move ahead on the global security agenda. Alone, it will always encounter American resistance, but working in a strong partnership of like-minded nations — each of which also needs the benefits of solidarity with other states — a great influence can be brought to bear on Washington. Canada's leading role in pushing the Western nuclear states toward a ban on land mines illustrates that it can build an international consensus — when it decides to act.

If these ten important middle powers together asked the American Administration to take seriously a NWC, it would shore up public opinion now evolving in the United States. A 1997 Abolition 2000 poll showed that 84 per cent of Americans would feel safer knowing that no country, including their own, had nuclear weapons. Might not the Administration, facing hostile elements in Congress that drive and intimidate the decision-making process, actually welcome, and be strengthened by, the outside pressure of moderate middle-powers that command the respect of the American public? The abolition of nuclear weapons will demand innovative action by key middle powers exercising their responsibility for global governance through preventive diplomacy. Such countries need to open up a dialogue with the United States and the other nuclear states to identify and analyze the political requirements for abolition. What are these requirements? Are they justified? Or are they just being used in some quarters as excuses for retaining the status quo?

PART THREE

The Moral Case Against Nuclear Weapons

8

The Real Reason for
Nuclear Weapons

What is the real reason behind the nuclear states' refusal to let go of
their nuclear weapons? Is not the logic of abolition overpowering?
The Cold War is over, and there is no longer any superpower "enemy." Nuclear weapons have been virtually repudiated by the World
Court. They have no military use, threaten the existence of life on
the planet, and undermine harmonious international relations needed
to resolve new threats to global security — mass poverty and environmental degradation. Nuclear deterrence justifies military build-
ups and has not preserved peace. Nuclear weapons contradict every
goal of the United Nations. What, then, is holding back the advance
into a nuclear-weapon-free world?

There are two broad categories of problems that block abolition.
I call them *on-the-table* problems and *under-the-table* problems. The
former are discussed quite openly; the latter are seldom referred to.

On-the-table problems have two main divisions: technical and
political. Nuclear anarchy presents a technical challenge that has not
yet been resolved. Civil stocks of plutonium used for nuclear power
are growing enormously. Reactor-grade plutonium and highly enriched uranium can be used for nuclear weapons. Even with international safeguards, as long as such stocks remain under national
control they could be subject to political upheaval or changes in
national strategy. A process of political disintegration, such as that
experienced by the former Soviet Union and Yugoslavia, could recur
in a nuclear state, exposing stores of separated plutonium, fresh
plutonium-bearing fuel, or highly-enriched uranium to seizure by
contending political forces or sale to organized criminal elements,
other governments, and sub-national groups. The potential for the
diversion of civil stocks that are inherently capable of being promptly

made into nuclear weapons will make military establishments reluctant to reduce their own stockpiles. In other words, the nuclear powers can always argue that they could never be sure that weapon-capable nuclear material in other states will never be used for bombs, and so they have to keep a basic number of nuclear weapons as a deterrent.

The accelerating demand for nuclear energy represents a "plutonium economy" of the future that inhibits abolition. Repeated thefts of fissile material in Russia is a harbinger of what might come if the present pattern of national controls and less-than-perfect safeguards is maintained. International ownership and management of all stocks of weapon-capable material is needed to guarantee it will never fall into the wrong hands. Such curbs would collide with market demands, and the major industrial states have shown no willingness to be so hampered. However, sooner or later, the most stringent international control over all fissile material will have to be accepted.

The nuclear states claim that stolen fissile material could be acquired by a terrorist group and used to produce a bomb. This can never be discounted, but if a terrorist organization did wish to kill on a mass scale, biological, or even chemical, weapons would be a likelier choice than nuclear ones, since they are both simpler and less expensive to make. The problem of terrorism is growing, but maintaining nuclear weapons cannot help resolve it. How could a state retaliate against terrorists with nuclear weapons? The very idea of using nuclear weapons to attack terrorists in the middle of a populous centre is absurd. Retention of nuclear weapons is likely to *increase*, rather than *decrease*, the risks of nuclear terrorism. The creation of a de-nuclearized world would de-legitimize nuclear weapons and thus reduce the ability of anyone to acquire them.

The status of international regimes to eliminate other weapons of mass destruction is another technical obstacle to a nuclear-weapon-free world. How certain can the nuclear states be that all chemical and biological weapons, banned under existing international treaties, will in fact be destroyed? In the absence of a credible process for their destruction, the nuclear powers could decide they need nuclear weapons to deter chemical and biological attacks. The negative security assurances they have given — not to use nuclear weapons against non-nuclear nations — are not accepted as legally binding. At the present stage of international law, a state contemplating a chemical or biological attack could never be sure it might not suffer a nuclear bombing in retaliation. A robust verification regime to ensure that chemical and biological weapons are not being produced anywhere will be necessary before the nuclear powers will let go of their nuclear weapons.

Obviously, international confidence must be built at each successive step along the way by showing that the new arrangements are promoting, not detracting from, security. Verification establishes whether all parties are complying with their obligations under an agreement, and the success of any agreement depends on building an atmosphere of trust. This trust can only be maintained if all sides are aware that cheating is likely to be detected. Verification cannot provide 100-percent certainty, but after several years of monitoring and inspection in the area of chemical and biological weapons, and with the transition to low levels of nuclear weapons, a pattern of knowledge would be built up, so confidence in the process would be high. If a non-nuclear state tried to create a clandestine program to build nuclear weapons, the activities of reactors, even if underground, would be detected by remote infra-red sensors. A properly financed and staffed verification agency, operating with the full cooperation of all the nuclear states, would make it unacceptably dangerous for any party to cheat on an agreement. If the verification provisions of an agreement are comprehensive, then parties will be deterred from cheating, because they know they run a high risk of getting caught. This is called "verification deterrence."

The possibility of "breakout" is another technical reason why the nuclear powers have refused to countenance complete nuclear disarmament. There is a concern that an existing nuclear power could cheat by retaining a secret cache of nuclear weapons or fissile material. While it is true that such a cache might escape external detection, no state contemplating cheating could be certain that its transgression would not be revealed from within. Any cheating would be known to a considerable number of citizens. While governments can legitimately require citizens to keep secrets relating to *lawful* national security concerns, they cannot require them to break international laws. If just one individual refused to go along with the deception and "blew the whistle," all would be revealed. A deviant government could never be sure that it would not be exposed from within. "Breakout" would involve real risks of being caught and provoking international action against the offending State.

Even if no conceivable verification system could give absolute assurance against the clandestine development of a nuclear weapon somewhere, it would be far less dangerous than the current risk of proliferation. Intrusive verification is the key to the success of the Intermediate Nuclear Forces Treaty, under which American and Russian inspectors are now permitted on each other's soil to monitor the dismantling of intermediate-range nuclear weapons. The Chemical Weapons Convention also provides for intrusive inspection. These systems can be replicated. The United Nations has done several verification studies that point to the feasibility of a comprehensive international verification system. Disarmament is expensive (which seems to surprise some politicians) but it is infinitely cheaper than both war and keeping today's highly sophisticated weaponry in a state of readiness. The political process must be encouraged to spare no resources to assure a high-confidence verification regime.

The technical on-the-table problems, though complex, are not insurmountable, given the political will to solve them. But the political will is not present because the nuclear powers want to keep their nuclear weapons for political reasons.

The U.S. Is the Key

When we speak of the nuclear powers in a political context, we must narrow our focus primarily to the United States. China has committed itself to a time-bound abolition program. Russia, emerging from the Cold War, has sought nuclear elimination, but hard-line elements in its military and political establishments fear humiliation brought on by economic collapse and insist on retaining nuclear weapons as a symbol of power. NATO's expansion has not only slowed Russian ratification of START II, it has also reinforced Russian determination to face up to American strength by retaining its nuclear weapons. Britain and France are holding onto their nuclear arsenals to bolster their political standing as they jockey for power in the new Europe, but their position would be untenable if Washington made an unequivocal commitment to go to zero. It is the United States that is in a decisive position: it is the Western leader, the lynchpin of NATO, and by far the strongest military power in the world. In any weapons negotiations, the Americans deal from a position of strength.

Washington holds that there are two classes of threats to which nuclear weapons remain important deterrents. First, since Russia continues to possess substantial strategic nuclear forces and an even larger stockpile of tactical nuclear weapons, the United States feels threatened. It fears that the deterioration of Russia's conventional military capabilities might force Moscow to place even more reliance on its nuclear forces. The future of Russian politics is so cloudy that Washington thinks it may one day again have to deter Russia's nuclear force.

This argument can be met by turning the situation around. Suppose Russia had won the Cold War and the United States was disintegrating economically: Russia now maintained its dominant position in the world through its nuclear arsenal. Would not Washington then keep its nuclear weapons in an effort to maintain its international status? Now come back to reality. How can the United States expect Russia to unilaterally give up its nuclear weapons when NATO has determined that nuclear weapons are "essential," when Washington is forging ahead with development of a ballistic missile-defence system, when the Americans have stated that nuclear deterrence is a permanent policy? The onus is on the United States to reassure Russia, with concrete action, that nuclear weapons have no place in a post-Cold War security partnership. When that assurance is given, both sides can work together to get to zero. Such a plan would start by joint action toward a "zero-alert" posture.

The second American concern involves the potential nuclear threat from what they call "rogue states." Washington believes that knowledge of a powerful and ready nuclear capability is a significant deterrent to would-be proliferators. It believes that the Saddam Husseins, the Muammar Kaddafis and the Kim Chong Ils of the world are deterred from developing their own nuclear weapons only by a reliable and flexible American nuclear capability, and so it would be irresponsible to dismantle that capability before new and reliable systems for preserving stability are in place.

This argument is met by the recognition that vertical proliferation — the policy of the nuclear states to add to and perfect their arsenals — has been a major reason why other states have tried to develop nuclear weapons. They confer prestige. The link between possession of nuclear weapons and a permanent seat on the U.N. Security Council must be broken. Would-be nuclear states must be convinced, first, that the nuclear powers are genuinely moving to zero, and second, that going nuclear would vastly exacerbate any regional disputes they may be involved in. Here, the international community must give much stronger backing to the U.N.'s conflict-mediation procedures. Because of its strength, the United States can provide the leadership needed to encourage all states to foster dialogue, openness, and other trust- and confidence-building measures with their neighbours. This would be a more reliable and effective means of providing global security than confrontation or deterrence. A credible American commitment to a nuclear-weapon-free world would encourage other states to strengthen collective and cooperative means of addressing their security concerns. The process of eliminating nuclear weapons would enhance the possibility of developing a global cooperative security system. If the United Nations could be built out of the ashes of World War II, so too an international agency to keep the peace can be developed out of the Cold War experience.

The United States still appears convinced its nuclear weapons do not stimulate "rogue states" to catch up. It believes instead that their effort to obtain nuclear weapons stems from a desire to counter regional adversaries, to further regional ambitions, and to enhance their status among their neighbours. Only American possession of nuclear weapons and their readiness to use them in retaliation against a "rogue state" deters such proliferation. In this posture, Washington is the world cop, stick in hand. This view amounts to autocracy. If there is anything the world should have learned from the twentieth century, it is that the era of dictators, benign or otherwise, is over. There is always a reaction against a dictator. Security today cannot be obtained by domination: rather, a system of enforceable international law developed through cooperation — not threat — is the only viable course. The United States is not confident such a system can be built: its friends must help it to re-think its position.

Washington rejects the claim that nuclear weapons are unsafe, too susceptible to accidental or unauthorized use. Conceding that accidents involving nuclear weapons have occured in the past, it believes its weapons meet the highest standards of safety, security, and responsible custodianship. Further, the safety risks of maintaining its current nuclear arsenal are far outweighed by the security benefits the country continues to derive from nuclear deterrence. The recklessness of such logic was roundly criticized by the Canberra Commission:

> The proposition that larger numbers of nuclear weapons can
> be retained in perpetuity and never used — accidentally or
> by decision — defies credibility.

Despite elaborate systems of control, the fatal flaw of nuclear deterrence is that if it fails, it will do so with catastrophic consequences. The most elaborate safety systems cannot overcome human fallibility. Accidents have happened before. The lives of countless people and future generations would be devastated and the environment savaged if another accident got out of control. What right does Washington have to take such chances with the well-being of humanity?

Finally, the United States believes there is no reasonable prospect that all the declared and *de facto* nuclear powers will agree, in the near term, to give up all their nuclear weapons. As long as only one state refuses to do so, Washington argues, it will be necessary to retain an American nuclear force. Even if the nuclear powers were to accept abolition, the difficulties of maintaining an enforceable verification system in a time of political tension or crisis would be insurmountable. Moreover, the world is still heavily armed with conventional weapons and thus, nuclear weapons are needed to discourage the resort to force.

Again, such arguments ignore the knowledge gained from the Cold War and reflect the militarist mentality that peace can only come out of the barrel of a gun. This mentality is short-sighted, pessimistic, and produces a profound despair among people who feel that the powerful have learned nothing from twentieth-century history. The world has lived under the mushroom cloud since 1945 and the cumulative psychological impact has been overwhelmingly negative. If the United States is determined to retain its nuclear weapons, at least until every last conventional weapon in the world has been laid down, then no amount of counter-argument or planning for a nuclear-weapon-free world will satisfy it.

Power and Racism

Arguments about these on-the-table problems keep going round and round. They all involve, at their centre, one word: security. But that is not the real reason the Western nuclear powers are so adamant. Their opposition to abolition stems from another word: power. Power is the under-the-table reason. The "enemy" that Western nuclear states train their nuclear weapons on is not another country, but the potential loss of the power by which they control the world economy. Nuclear weapons are for the protection of the Western way of life against the rising clamour of the disenfranchised of the world, who increasingly resent being exploited.

Let me explain my views this way. As a young man journeying around the world, through Africa, Asia, and Latin America, I made what seemed to me, given my parochial background, an amazing discovery: most of the world is non-white, non-Western, and non-Christian. The world is full of people who have had to cope with being politically, economically, and socially discriminated against by Western power systems and patronized by Western religions. One great example illustrates this massive discrimination. The one-fifth of humanity living in the West ("the North" in economic terms) controls 75 percent of the wealth, resources, and capital in the world: the other fourth-fifths of humanity, "the South," has to make do with the remaining 25 percent, and the gap between rich and poor continues to widen. In 1960, the richest fifth of humanity was thirty times as wealthy as the poorest fifth. By 1990, it was sixty times as wealthy.

In the 1970s, the non-aligned countries, which make up a great majority of the world's peoples, recognized that political liberation had not given them the human security they yearned for, and they demanded a "new international economic order." A document with this title appeared, calling for negotiations between North and South on such crucial instruments of the world economy as resources, energy, capital, and development assistance. The North would agree to such negotiations only if they were held under the umbrella of the International Monetary Fund and World Bank, both of which the North controls. The South wanted negotiations in the General Assembly, where their weight of numbers would count. No relevant negotiations ever took place: the "new international economic order" died before it was born.

Following the Gulf War of 1991, another "new world order" was talked about in the West. What was meant was that the centre of power would be in Washington, not the United Nations. The ensuing disorder of the 1990s has buried the notion of a "new world order" centred around the United Nations. Nonetheless, the clamour for equality is growing, showing up in all the debates over human rights, economic growth, and now nuclear weapons. Already, we can see that the defining problem of the early twenty-first century will be the struggle for equity — between and among all nations, between and among all peoples.

The basis of the South's claim to equality is that every human being has a right to development, which means the right to have access to those goods and instruments necessary for the provision of basic human needs. The North has resisted this through the years because of what it perceives as the consequences: a sharing of resources rather than control over them. The common heritage of the seas is but one example: one of the reasons the Law of the Sea has been so watered down is that major states have refused to recognize that the minerals, which constitute a vast amount of wealth in the common areas of the ocean floor, should be shared. The sharing provisions of the Law of the Sea, as it was originally written, have now been changed to allow the major powers to go in with their high technology, extract the resources, and become even richer. The concepts of sharing and stewardship of the planet so necessary to common security continue to be resisted by the North.

As the stress on the ecosphere worsens — brought about by a combination of large populations and poverty in the South and over-consumption and pollution in the North — the demand of marginalized peoples for their place in the sun will grow. The image of mendicant beggars is already giving way to one of strident demanders working their way up the ladder of market economies. The military capacity of countries normally thought of as poor is surprisingly strong. Some thirty-five non-NATO countries already have non-nuclear ballistic missiles, including Algeria, Belarus, Kazakhstan, Egypt, India, Pakistan, Israel, and Saudi Arabia. Nearly twenty non-NATO countries are capable of installing either nuclear, biological, or chemical warheads.

In the face of pressures bound only to increase in the early years of the next century — pressures of the poor and homeless demanding resources and space, pressures of regional disputes over scarce commodities (of which fresh water will likely be at the head of the list), pressures growing out of the resentment against the white, Christian West for hogging the lion's share of the world's benefits (an imbalance made ever more visible through the exploding communications revolution), pressures from the ambitious military of the South — nuclear proponents will stand their ground. They will never admit that fear of the rise of the non-white, non-Western, and non-Christian peoples of the world, fueled by fundamentalist elements that scorn political accommodation and religious ecumenism as but code words for the philosophy of domination, has anything to do with maintaining the doctrine of nuclear deterrence. Nuclear weapons are needed, they will argue, not necessarily to use, but to threaten those who would challenge the Western way of life. The British implied exactly this thinking in a 1995 Defence White Paper that threatened limited nuclear strikes to defend vital interests, which were defined as trade, the sea routes used for it, raw materials from abroad, and overseas British investment. There might not be enough of everything needed to sustain Western lifestyles — land, resources, wealth. Who knows what might happen? All the problems surrounding the basic needs of humans on a planet with definable limitations of growth are only getting worse. The turbulence of today could become the gales of tomorrow, and so — according to the nuclear powers — nuclear weapons are necessary to protect the West against the unknown forces of the next century.

Nuclear proponents would never express their beliefs in terms of racism, and they should not be accused of racism, *per se*, any more than a person who buys a fur coat should be denigrated as an animal-hater. Many nuclear adherents are undoubtedly anti-racist (just as nuclear abolitionists are not all, by definition, multiculturalists). There is, however, a racist element in the Western attitude to the rest of the world, and it has manifested itself through colonialism, economic domination, and nuclear weapons. Along with the people of Japan, who suffered atomic devastation, the indigenous and colonized peoples of the South Pacific have also reaped bitter nuclear fruit through the mining of uranium and the testing of nuclear weapons on indigenous peoples' lands, the dumping, storage, and transport of plutonium and nuclear wastes, and the seizure of land for nuclear infrastructure. Superiority is the basic characteristic of the Westerner contemplating the rest of the world. The fact that non-white and non-Christian China, powerful and feared by the West, possesses nuclear weapons only encourages those in favour of nuclear retention to argue all the harder.

The official American position on nuclear weapons is not, of course, embraced by the totality of the American people. Nor is the American government a monolith, though the Administration must take full responsibility for the key decision to maintain nuclear deterrence. There are competing viewpoints throughout the American structure, but current foreign policy is driven by an ideological, right-wing element that is itself fearful of a non-white, non-Western, non-Christian world. Such fear is then spread through a populace numbed by the ceaseless crises of the post-Cold War era, which have brought mayhem rather than peace. In this view, the world is out of control, and only a strong American hand can set it straight. In this mindset, the United Nations is discounted and undermined: only the political domination and military might of the West, led by the United States, can save the world (meaning the West) from uncontrollable forces.

Nuclear weapons are a racist tool that a placid public has accepted as necessary (although not so many, please) because the public has never adjusted its thinking from the Cold War. Within the United States, there are important organizations and numerous activists trying to influence the national viewpoint. The Henry L. Stimson Center, the Center for Defense Information, the Monterey Institute of International Studies, and the Nuclear Age Peace Foundation are among the prestigious, non-partisan research centres warning that the uncertainties of the world can only be adequately dealt with if the nuclear powers commit themselves in earnest to the dedicated pursuit of a world without nuclear weapons. The prestigious National Academy of Sciences has called for the United States and Russia to reduce their arsenals to "a few hundred each" and has advised the Administration that the potential benefits of a global ban on nuclear weapons "warrant serious efforts to identify and promote the conditions that would make this work." But voices of reason are drowned in an ongoing welter of political rhetoric abetted by the media's endless fascination with the confrontational and the trivial. The propaganda that nuclear weapons won the Cold War (an assumption already losing its credibility as analytical research deepens) is brazenly trumpeted by nuclear proponents. They diminish logic, language, and the law in their determination to hold on to the past.

One justification for nuclear weapons can no longer be claimed: morality. The nakedness of their violence against humanity is now exposed, and they have lost every last vestige of any claim to morality.

9

Recognizing Moral Bankruptcy

Nuclear weapons are the ultimate evil. The nuclear powers would not be able to so blithely carry on with their nuclear weapons programs if world consciousness, raised to a new recognition of this evil, demanded abolition. But world consciousness has been dulled. We have lived with the bomb so long that it has insinuated itself into our thinking. Hiroshima and Nagasaki seem so long ago, they are but a blur in memory. Anyway, "They can't happen again." The sheer horror of nuclear devastation has been veiled from people's minds.

Media and political processes ignore the centrality of the nuclear issue: evil. When they do deal with nuclear weapons, it is usually in terms of deterring an "enemy." The Cold War language continues into the new era: the old euphemisms of "nuclear preparedness" and "collateral damage" continue to hide the real issues of extermination by the million, incineration while the populations of cities, genetic deformities, inducement of cancers, destruction of the food chain, and the imperiling of civilization. And so the calamity awaiting humanity — that is, an extraordinarily grave event marked by great loss and lasting distress and affliction — is concealed.

The abolition movement seeks to open the eyes of society to this evil, and society is not impervious to evil: the Holocaust, AIDS, and genocide have all been recognized as the evils they are. But the ultimate — last, final, most remote in time or space — evil appears to be too far removed from daily life to engage our attention.

It is almost as if the issue is too big to handle. Nuclear weapons assault life on the planet, they assault the planet itself, and in so doing they assault the process of the continuing development of the planet. This is an affront to God, the Creator of the universe, an affront to the mysterious process of creation that makes a connection between us and an unfathomably distant past that the present generation has no right to interrupt. Nuclear weapons rival the power of God. They challenge God. They lure us into thinking we can control the destiny of the world. They turn upside down the natural morality that ensues from the relationship between God and humanity. Nuclear weapons are evil, because they destroy the process of life itself. They invert order into disorder.

Nuclear weapons are supposed to be governed by the covenants of humanitarian law. In fact, a nuclear war would destroy the very basis of humanitarian law. The structure of our civilization would disappear. Nuclear weapons, with no limitation or proportionality in their effect, make a mockery of old "just war" theories. How can self-defence be cited as a justification for the use of nuclear weapons when their full effect destroys the "self" that is supposed to be defended?

Our Complicity in Violence

Nuclear weapons will only be abolished when the moral consciousness of humanity is raised, just as it was raised by the moral re-assessment and rejection of slavery, colonialism, and apartheid.

The moral case against nuclear weapons begins with recognition of our willingness to commit violence. The world is filled with violence. People are attacked on the streets, in their homes, even in institutions where the horrors of sexual abuse have now come to light. Great sections of humanity are economically discriminated against and even robbed of their right to basic human needs. Violence is so endemic in our culture that it has become routine. We are numbed by it. It floods the entertainment media, and we even pay to see it. It produces a bored reaction in newscasts. The political lobby that fights gun control reflects the vengeance that is handmaiden to violence. Pervasive violence has made us both fearful and apathetic at the same time. We now know so much about the world that the tortures, beatings, rapes, killings, and genocidal slaughters that assault us daily have produced a social ennui. We are essentially helpless against this corrosive force — so let's just get on with life.

Violence, however, is not an inevitable part of human nature, just as war is not necessarily an inescapable phenomenon of history. It is scientifically incorrect to say violent behaviour is genetically programmed into our human nature. Violence is neither in our evolutionary legacy nor in our genes, and there is nothing in our neurophysiology that compels us to act violently. Nor is the nation-state necessarily warlike. Sweden and Japan are two nations, both with warring pasts, that pride themselves on their efforts for peace. Nobel Peace laureate Joseph Rotblat points out that violence in modern wars is often mistaken as the cause, rather than the consequence, of the process:

> Biology does not condemn humanity to war. Just as wars begin in the minds of men, peace also begins in our minds. The same species which invented war is capable of inventing peace. The responsibility lies with each of us.

Wars are, of course, political decisions, but they also require technological means, which through history have ranged from the club to the nuclear bomb. One cannot have war without arms, and if we are serious about preventing war, we must end their production. It is the official policy of governments to curb the arms trade, but governments actually encourage arms exports for financial gain. It is not a big leap from toleration of the arms trade to acquiescence in the resulting violence, and nuclear weapons are the ultimate violence.

We do not want violence done to ourselves, yet we do it to others. This shocking dichotomy ought to awaken us to reciprocity, a universally valid moral value. As Confucius taught: "What you do not want done to yourself, do not do to others." The rule of reciprocity is defined by followers of Christ as The Golden Rule. On the eve of the twenty-first century, this means that governments should take as a starting point in the formulation of their policies the impact of those policies on other states. As the doctrine of nuclear deterrence so pointedly illustrates, one nation's *security* can mean another's *insecurity*. Mountains of U.N. documents on global security can be summed up by the simple dictum: states should treat others as they wish to be treated in return.

Reciprocity may not lay claim to a high level of altruism, but it is a valid and effective base on which to find and express human values for common security. Reciprocity has certainly moved from the realm of idealism to the most basic realism: survival. Here we find common ground between spirituality and technology: what spirituality tells us we ought to do (love one another) technology tells us we must do so we do not destroy one another. If love is deemed by some to be too strong (given the ideological, cultural, and racial divides that still exist) at least acceptance and tolerance are demanded as the price of life, liberty, and happiness in a world that has become one. If we need reminding of the oneness of the world and the integrity of all life, look again at that first photo of the planet sent back by the Apollo astronauts: beautiful, fragile, one. In previous centuries, we did not even know one another, let alone care about each other. Now, technology has united us, at least in our knowledge of one another.

Through the United Nations and its systems, we possess, for the first time in the history of the world, a catalogue of information about how our planet works, and we have developed treaties to protect the rights of individuals and the environment itself. Both people and governments are learning that they must cooperate for many purposes — to maintain peace and order, to expand economic activity, to tackle pollution, to halt or minimize climate change, to combat disease, to curb the proliferation of weapons, to prevent desertification, to preserve genetic and species diversity, to deter terrorists, to ward off famines.

A New Global Ethic

All this has prepared us for the formulation of a new global ethic. By "global ethic," I do not mean a global ideology or a single unified religion, and I certainly don't mean the domination of one religion at the expense of others. Rather, I mean a fundamental consensus on binding values, irrevocable standards, and personal attitudes. This ethic is the expression of a vision of peoples living peacefully together, of national and ethnic groupings of people sharing responsibility for the care of the planet. The abolition of nuclear weapons must become a central part of this new global ethic of enlightened realism.

It is interesting that the Report of the Commission on Global Governance, after its opening chapter describing the post-Cold War world, turned immediately to an elaboration of "Values for the Global Neighbourhood":

> We believe that all humanity could uphold the core values of respect for life, liberty, justice and equity, mutual respect, caring, and integrity. These provide a foundation for transforming a global neighbourhood based on economic exchange and improved communications into a universal moral community in which people are bound together by more than proximity, interest, or identity. They all derive in one way or another from the principle, which is in accord with relig-

ious teachings around the world, that people should treat others as they would themselves wish to be treated.

The Commission urged the international community to unite in support of a global ethic of common rights and shared responsibilities. This would "provide the moral foundation for constructing a more effective system of global governance" and close the present gap between governments and citizens. A global civic ethic would also require democratic and accountable institutions and the rule of law.

Discussions on ethics frequently become esoteric, not to mention divisive. But a new global ethic can be expressed sharply, succinctly, and irrefutably, as the 1993 Parliament of the World's Religions did: "Every human being must be treated humanely!"

This echoed a dramatic appeal contained in a 1955 manifesto issued by a group of scientists led by Bertrand Russell and Albert Einstein who, having worked on the development of the atomic bomb, called for its abolition: "We appeal, as human beings, to human beings: Remember your humanity, and forget the rest."

Voicing a Moral Concern

There have been numerous contemporary calls for an ethical response to the planet's problems. One of the most notable of these came from a U.N.-sponsored seminar on the ethical and spiritual dimensions of social progress, held as part of preparations for the World Summit for Social Development. Convened at Bled, Slovenia, in October 1994, the thirty-five delegates sought to advance a common ethical understanding of poverty, employment, and social integration, and to "pave the way for a more holistic perception of international cooperation." The U.N., being by definition a place where it is hard to find a common denominator, has customarily avoided discussions of spirituality, even though two of its Secretaries-General, Dag Hammarskjold and U Thant, were intensely religious men. But this seminar took as a working assumption that spirituality is an integral part of reality, and that compassion, altruism, and generosity have the power to move societies away from fear, despair, selfishness, arrogance, and violence. It criticized the "social Darwinism" spreading through the world as the strong, getting stronger, marginalize the weak:

The same Promethean philosophy, deriving from a concept of Man as master of the universe, has resulted in extensive damage to the planet and destruction of its wealth. In addition to the dangers which this situation presents for the survival of humankind, it demonstrates a lack of respect for the environment which is related to the various forms of violence afflicting contemporary societies.

Fundamental freedoms and civil and political rights represent basic achievements of humanity, "but individual freedom is meaningless and dangerous when not rooted in an ethic and enlightened by the Spirit." Human dignity, "the very nature of the human being as created by God," must be safeguarded by political action and the exercise of power. Thus a new ethic, based on hope rather than fear, should make it possible to transcend the world's differences. "This moral and spiritual renewal is a matter of urgency."

Throughout the Cold War, moral teaching on nuclear weapons was uncertain. While some ethicists condemned outright the concept of nuclear deterrence as a crime against God and humanity, others gave limited acceptance to the possession of nuclear weapons in the genuine belief that they were an aid to peace. Recognition of the ultimate evil took a back seat to the immediate gain of preventing nuclear conflict. There was a great deal of twisting and turning, as religious leaders tried to reconcile the opposing demands of natural law and political realism. Moral constraints had to compete with "reasons of state." The tensions between them got caught up in the old religious arguments about passivism and "just war". The barrage of propaganda about Soviet forces about to charge the Western gates skewed, or at least intimidated, a moral consensus on the evil of nuclear weapons.

Political acceptance of nuclear weapons to deter "the enemy" became the over-riding consideration. When the Soviets disappeared as the enemy, the nuclear establishment had to find a new one. This time the enemy is some political leader, now or in the future, who will threaten the West with a nuclear weapon. The circle of fear, perpetuated by those with a vested interest in maintaining nuclear weapons, is unending. Unchallenged, this is a trap humanity will never escape from.

The moral challenge to nuclear weapons remains weak. It is almost as if moralists are afraid to moralize, as if the argument of immorality loses its impact in a secular world, as if stamping out evil can't compete with scientific advancement. The world ethos is clearly weak in legislating and enforcing the protection of the common good. This is all the more reason for ethicists to speak out, to reach down into the depths of their humanity to decry the very instruments that attack humanity. This is not "moralism," it is not "rhetoric," it is not "simplism." It is, rather, the recovery of a teaching that human conscience must assert itself in any understanding of right and wrong. To fail to do this is to consign humanity to denigration of intellect and loss of will, to deny it the very essence of humanity.

The Western nuclear powers must be challenged, for, in clinging to spurious, self-serving rationales, they are deliberately deceiving the world. The gravest of futures lies ahead for humanity if the world is to be ruled by militarism rather than law. The doctrine of nuclear deterrence can no longer claim the slightest shred of moral acceptance: it is morally bankrupt. The dangers of proliferation make it essential that religious leaders teach, with one voice, that nuclear weapons are immoral. Nuclear planners would then be deprived of any further claim to moral legitimacy.

The nuclear powers may not immediately heed a clear moral condemnation of nuclear weapons, just as they have tried to brush off the World Court's Advisory Opinion. But the force of morality and law cannot long be ignored if the peoples of the world build their case for abolition on these twin bases.

Nuclear weapons are no longer about the enemy. Nuclear weapons *are* the enemy. They do not prevent evil: they *are* evil, in its most devastating form.

10

Deciding to Hope

Hiroshima taught me hope. That may seem incongruous, given the devastation and suffering the city endured, but Hiroshima has pushed ahead into new life, not wallowed in despair. This hopeful spirit struck me forcibly on a visit there in 1983. With my wife Eva and our friends Walter and Barbara McLean, I spent a day visiting the museum in the city's Peace Memorial Park, with its vivid, even electrifying, depictions of atomic horror. I interviewed some of the survivors and heard tales of unimaginable personal suffering. The day was one of unremitting gloom.

The four of us went back to our hotel, a modern edifice on a traffic-filled street, and sank into chairs in the lobby. Celebration was the furthest thing from our minds, but a grand piano occupied a corner of the lobby, a pianist began to play Broadway cocktail music, and our spirits began to pick up. The concierge came by and told us a baseball game would start in an hour — Hiroshima against Tokyo. On an impulse, we took a taxi to the stadium, bought baseball caps, and got caught up in the enthusiasm, even frenzy, of the hometown crowd cheering for Hiroshima. By the end of the game (it ended in a tie!) we'd learned the rhythms of the Japanese chants and performed them exuberantly.

Afterwards, we reflected on the good time we'd had. The evening had not been frivolous but it had offered us a release from the horror of the day and allowed our minds to focus on the future. Hiroshima had re-built itself: life went on. Hope for a better future was in the air.

If the people of Hiroshima can have hope, I've often told myself, so can I. Being of Irish descent, I have a streak of blackness in me: sometimes I feel that the forces of evil are just too much, and that they will triumph over goodness, because evil seems to be so much more insistent on getting its way than goodness does. Every weapon ever made has been used. The refinement of killing goes on in the minds of scientists, in the policies of governments, and in the factories of arms merchants. Greed is so dominant a human characteristic that the powerful demand weapons to protect themselves, while the marginalized demand weapons to overcome their oppression. The circle of death goes on and cannot be stopped: humanity, fallen, cannot lift itself out of the abyss. Nuclear weapons, the ultimate evil, win: humanity loses.

I do have such thoughts, and I would be false to this book if I did not admit it. But I overcome them by recognizing the blossoming of intelligence that is a chief characteristic of our time. We are not fated to oblivion. We are not lost in a jungle at midnight without a compass. Our world has become a human community inter-connected in every sphere of activity. This is an empowering discovery, and is capable of enervating the process of public policy formation. And it is. The United Nations, the World Court, and a myriad of regional institutions reveal humanity's organizational ability to move forward in creating structures for a peaceful life.

Hope has overcome fear in my own life. I have perhaps been helped in this by recalling that hope is one of the three great theological virtues. (Faith and love are the other two.) Hope must become more than a poor cousin to the powerhouses of faith and love. Elusive and mysterious, hope has the capacity to powerfully influence individual and social behaviour.

Hope Is a Verb

Hope is much more than a bridging word signifying a wish for something we cannot control: "I *hope* the weather will be warm tomorrow." Hope is more than a passive shrug: "Let's *hope* for the best." Hope is more than a blind assumption that things will turn out all right. Hope is best understood as a verb, connoting an active desire with the expectation of fulfillment: we long for something, and will it to happen. Hope, of course, cannot guarantee that we get what we long for, but it activates us in the search, and provides a pathway from vision to reality. Hope, weaving itself like an essential thread through thoughts and experiences that speak of the human condition, is the great motivater. The bigger the dream, the stronger must be the hope. Through hope, we overcome.

There are signs of hope that the abolition of nuclear weapons can be achieved, despite what appear to be intractable forces of opposition. The first of these signs is knowledge or, more strictly, the power of knowledge. We know more about the planet and how it works than ever before. Over the past two decades, global conferences of the United Nations have produced a catalogue of information on every world subject from food and energy to population and pollution. That first photo of the Earth sent back from outer space symbolizes this knowledge: we can see ourselves as a whole people, on common ground.

A second sign that there is hope for abolition is the explosive growth of civil society movements. Activists for social change are sometimes referred to as NGOs — members of non-governmental organizations. There are at least 250 million members of non-governmental organizations around the world. The leaders of these groups, specializing in such subjects as disarmament, development, environmental protection, and human rights, have developed a global presence that stimulates, encourages, reprimands, and otherwise pressures governments toward forward-minded global security policies. The NGO activists who gathered at the Earth Summit in Rio in 1992, the women who met at the Women's Conference in Beijing in 1995, the people of the Abolition 2000 movement, all are inspiring examples of the burgeoning civil society movement.

Many of these NGOs already have consultative status at the U.N., where they gather to inform and lobby national delegations. But they want more: they want to be within, not outside, the structures of power. A movement for a second chamber of the General Assembly is under study by leading-edge activists. This would provide delegates from around the world — they might even be elected for such a purpose — to come to the U.N. and formally propose, if not legislate, policies on global security issues. Secretary-General Annan's call for a "People's Millenium Assembly" at the U.N. in 2000 has boosted the status of the emerging society. The development of new, and the improvement of existing institutions that are moving in the direction of global governance is a third powerful sign of hope.

Much, perhaps most, of this ongoing work is obscured from public view by a media less interested in positive developments for change than in negative stories of confrontation and hateful things human beings still do to one another. Though media still drag us down, the creative activities of countless people, building on knowledge gained and now widely available on the Internet, account for the maturation of humanity now taking place.

Humanity's new awareness of itself is antidote to the ultimate evil. Vaclav Havel, President of the Czech Republic, puts it this way:

> If humanity has any hope of a decent future, it lies in the awakening of a universal sense of responsibility, the kind of responsibility unrepresented in the world of transient and temporal earthly interests.

An Attitude Towards Abolition

Like Havel, I cannot be sure political structures will take this path, but an emerging and dynamic civil society is leading to a human-rights-centred global democracy. The abolition movement must build on the new understanding of the integral nature of human rights in a technologically united world. Such an understanding will help us see that, in a world that is whole, my human rights are inextricably connected to the human rights of the Bosnian child, the Rwandan farmer, the Haitian worker. I must express a loyalty to these people, even if I do not personally know them, if I am to be true to myself.

In short, loyalty to all humanity means inculcating in people an *attitude,* not only to the world as it is, but as it can be. It means helping them understand the magnitude of the transformations taking place in the world. It means opening up their powers of creativity so that they don't just cope with the world, but enlarge the community around them. Unfortunately, the Cold War justification for nuclear weapons is so deeply imbedded in Western minds that the goal of a nuclear-weapon-free world requires, first of all, the re-education of electorates to teach them the goal is even possible. Abolitionists must confront "conventional wisdom."

The process of opening up the minds of the young to an awareness of the holistic nature of the planet should be a central concern of professional educators. Global education, properly done, can extend appreciation of one's own country *without* diminishing the people of other countries. There need not be a tension between educating for civic responsibility at home and educating for civic responsibility in a global context. Today, our community is, in fact, the world. I would go further: not to prepare young people for this kind of experience is to deny them the kind of education they will need in order to cope with the complexities of life ahead. A knowledge of history, an understanding of the evolving unity of the planet, a vision of social justice, and true human security are the essential qualities a human being needs in order to live peacefully in the twenty-first century.

Loyalty to all humanity has both a philosophical and pragmatic imperative that can be expressed and taught in a practical manner. A multi-dimensional agenda for world security has been defined by the United Nations: removal of threats to peace, including the nuclear threat; respect for the principle of the non-use of force; resolution of conflicts and peaceful settlement of disputes; confidence-building measures; disarmament; maintenance of outer space for peaceful uses; development; promotion of human rights and fundamental freedoms; the elimination of racial discrimination; enhancing the quality of life; satisfaction of human needs; and, protecting the environment.

A wide-ranging program of action is opened up by this definition. Action begins with an expression of the dictates of conscience to politicians, the media, our friends. Awakening of consciousness to the "ultimate evil" is a fundamental action with life-saving consequences. This approach, then, illuminates our comprehension that peace is established by the implementation of a system of values. Peace demands we attain true human security so people everywhere can live free of the threat of war, free of violations of their human rights, free to develop their own lives to attain economic and social progress. All this is clearly an advance in global thinking.

As global education widens its horizons, as civil society grows in strength and diversity, a synergy of human energy arising in a world of increased communication and transportation will enable new influences to be felt. This new kind of leadership, horizontally based, is far more promising of peace than is waiting for some new leader to appear on the mountaintop.

Patience is required, because today's turbulence has created an urgent situation. But I reject the thinking of such commentators as Freeman Dyson, who hold that the end of nuclear weapons is at least 100 years away and that until then "we must live with nuclear weapons as responsibly and quietly as we can." That is dangerous pessimism. The world does not have 100 years to stamp out this pernicious cancer that is eroding human security. There are too many people suffering, too much political frustration, too much potential for global devastation, to allow a mood of passivity. The abolition of nuclear weapons will not, by itself, bring peace, but it will allow the international community to deal more effectively with other threats to peace.

All great historical ideas for change go through three stages: first, the idea is ridiculed; then it is vigorously objected to; finally, it is accepted as conventional wisdom. The movement to abolish nuclear weapons has entered the second stage, as can be seen in the banner headline, "Don't Ban the Bomb," on the cover of a January, 1997 issue of the prestigious international journal *The Economist*.

The struggle to rid the world of nuclear weapons will be long and difficult: it is not for the faint-hearted. The opposition of those who, through ignorance, ideology, or greed, want to keep the status quo, will be vigorous, and perhaps ugly. But it cannot be denied that the historic momentum to contain, and then abolish, nuclear weapons is growing. We dare not lose our courage, our determination, our hope.

To hope for abolition means learning to think in a more human-centred way. To hope for abolition means putting the good of humanity in first place in public policy. To hope for abolition means committing ourselves, every day, to the further ascent of humanity.

Notes on Sources

Introduction: A New Sense of Urgency

A full discussion of the roundtables is contained in "Canada and the Abolition of Nuclear Weapons: A Window of Opportunity," published by Project Ploughshares, Institute of Peace and Conflict Studies, Conrad Grebel College, Waterloo, Ontario, N2L 3G6. Following presentation of this report to the Canadian government, the Parliamentary Committee on Foreign Affairs and International Trade was asked to begin a review of Canada's policies on nuclear weapons. With Ernie Regehr and Bill Robinson of Project Ploughshares, I testified at the Committee's opening hearing. Our brief can be found on the Project Ploughshares Web Site (watserv1.uwaterloo.ca/~plough/e18mar97.html).

Chapter 1: An Assault on Humanity

The stories told by Mayors Hiraoka and Itoh of the Hiroshima and Nagasaki bombings are taken from their testimony to the World Court in 1995. Judge Christopher Gregory Weeramantry, a member of the World Court, gave a separate opinion when the Court handed down its Advisory Opinion on the legality of nuclear weapons: in it is a detailed description of the effects of nuclear war. I have also drawn from "Study on the Climatic and other Global Effects of Nuclear War," published by the United Nations in 1988. The quotation from George Kennan is from his book *The Nuclear Delusion*, New York: Pantheon, 1982.

Chapter 2: The Proliferation of Nuclear Weapons

The Background Papers of the Canberra Commission on the Elimination of Nuclear Weapons contain a wealth of material on the present status of nuclear weapons. For information on the present stocks of the nuclear powers I have used "The Arsenals of the Nuclear Weapons Powers" by Christopher E. Paine, Thomas B.

Cochran and Robert S. Norris of the Natural Resources Defense Council. In describing the nuclear capabilities of other States, I have used "Nuclear Proliferation Outside the Nuclear Weapons States" by Leonard S. Spector, Carnegie Endowment for International Peace. I have also used two of Spector's other works, *Tracking Nuclear Proliferation, A Guide in Maps and Charts*, 1995, Washington, D.C.: Carnegie Endowment for International Peace, and *Nuclear Ambitions*, Boulder, Colorado; Westview Press. For the discussion on crises and accidents, I have used, with permission, two privately-circulated papers, "The Threats of Use of Nuclear Weapons During the Sixteen Known Nuclear Crises of the Cold War 1946-85," by David R. Morgan, National President, Veterans Against Nuclear Arms, and "Twenty Mishaps that Might Have Started Accidental Nuclear War," by Dr. Alan Phillips, Physicians for Global Survival. The Nuclear Control Institute, Washington, D.C. (Web Site: www.nci.org/nci/nci-nt.htm#opt1) publishes material on nuclear terrorism. The cost of nuclear weapons is explained in "Four Trillion Dollars and Counting," by the Nuclear Weapons Cost Study Project Committee, Ed: Stephen I. Schwartz, in *The Bulletin of the Atomic Scientists*, November-December 1995. The quotation from the U.S. Air Force Advisory Board is found in "New World Vistas: Air and Space Power for the 21st Century," 1996.

Chapter 3: Jeopardizing the Non-Proliferation Treaty

A full recounting of the 1995 NPT Review and Extension Conference is contained in my book, *An Unacceptable Risk: Nuclear Weapons in a Volatile World*, Project Ploughshares, 1995. India's full position on nuclear weapons is spelled out in David Cortright and Amitabh Mattoo (Eds.): *India and the Bomb: Public Opinion and Nuclear Options*, University of Notre Dame Press, 1996. The upgraded program of the International Atomic Energy Program is contained in "The IAEA's Programme '93+2'," by Suzanna Van Moyland, Verification Technology Information Centre. The argument for expanded power resources without relying on nuclear energy is found in "Energy After Rio: Prospects and Challenges," published by the United Nations Development Programme. The dangers of nuclear power are fully elaborated by the Nuclear Control Institute.

Chapter 4: The World Court's Legal Challenge

"The History of the World Court Project," by Kate Dewes and Robert Green, was published in *Pacifica Review*, Australia, Vol. 7, No. 2, October/November 1995. More background on the question the World Health Organization put to the World Court is in "Transnational Law and Contemporary Problems," published in *A Journal of the University of Iowa College of Law*, Vol. 4, No. 2, Fall 1994. I have also drawn from other analyses of the World Court's Advisory Opinion: Roger S. Clark and Madeline Sann,(Eds), *The Case Against the Bomb*, Rutgers University School of Law at Camden, New Jersey, 1996; J. Hatfield-Lyon, "The Legality of the Threat or Use of Nuclear Weapons: The Impact of the ICJ's Advisory Opinion on International Peace and Security," a paper presented at the 1996 Annual Conference of the Canadian Council on International Law; Peter Weiss, "Notes on a Misunderstood Decision: The World Court's Near Perfect Advisory Opinion in the Nuclear Weapons Case," a paper circulated by the Lawyers' Committee on Nuclear Policy, 666 Broadway, Room 625, New York, N.Y. 10012; Richard Falk, "Nuclear Weapons, International Law and the World Court: A Historic Encounter," published in *The American Journal of International Law*, Vol. 91, January 1997; "Implications of the Advisory Opinion By the International Court of Justice on the Legal Status of Nuclear Weapons," published by the World Court Project, 2 Chiswick House, High Street, Twyford, Berkshire, RG10 9AG; and, *International Review of the Red Cross*, Special Issue, January-February 1997. The full text of the Court's opinion and the separate statements of the judges are on the Internet (www.peacenet.org/disarm/icjtext.html).

Chapter 5: The Movement to Nuclear Zero

The Report of the Canberra Commission on the Elimination of Nuclear Weapons, published August 14, 1996, is available on the Internet (www.dfat.gov.au/dfat/cc/cchome.html). General Butler's comments are contained in *Disarmament Times*, published by the NGO Committee on Disarmament, March, 1997. A helpful addition to the Canberra Report is *Beyond the NPT: A Nuclear-Weapon-Free World*, published by the International Network of Engineers and Scientists Against Proliferation, April, 1995.

Chapter 6: The Outline of an Abolition Plan

I have used Benjamin B. Ferenz, *New Legal Foundations for Global Survival*, Oceana, 1994. The Moynihan quotation is from Daniel Patrick Moynihan, *On the Law of Nations*, Harvard University Press, 1990. I have used, with permission, "Nuclear Weapons, the International Court of Justice, and the Proposed International Criminal Court," an address by David Kreiger, President of the Nuclear Age Peace Foundation. The Group of 28 Program of Action was tabled at the Conference on Disarmament August 8, 1996. Three documents issued by the Lawyers Committee on Nuclear Policy explain the Model Nuclear Weapons Convention as well as providing the draft text, "Statement of Purpose"; "Text"; "Commentary." Material on verification and "breakout" was drawn from Patricia M. Lewis, "Verification Matters: Laying the Foundations," published by Verification Technology Information Centre, Carrara House, 20 Embankment Place, London WC2N 6NN, and Andrew Marck, "Nuclear 'Breakout'": Risks and Possible Responses," Background Papers, Canberra Commission.

Chapter 7: The Role of Middle Powers

The development of Parliamentarians for Global Action is detailed in my book, *Politicians for Peace*, Toronto: N.C. Press Limited, 1983. The Palme Report is published in the book *Common Security: A Blueprint for Survival*, New York: Simon and Schuster, 1982. The report of the Commission on Global Governance is published in the book, *Our Global Neighbourhood*, New York: Oxford University Press, 1995. The Final Document of the U.N. First Special Session on Disarmament is available through the United Nations Department of Public Information, Document DPI/679 — 40708, February, 1981. Boutros Boutros-Ghali's document *An Agenda for Peace*, is also available through the U.N.'s Department of Public Information. I have also drawn from "Canberra Follow-On," a paper presented by Jonathan Dean, Union of Concerned Scientists, to the NGO Forum, April 10, 1997.

Chapter 8: The Real Reason for Nuclear Weapons

A good description of technical and political problems surrounding nuclear weapons abolition is found in Christopher E. Paine, Thomas B. Cochran, Robert S. Norris, "Current Political Realities Facing the

Transition to a Nuclear-Weapon-Free World," published in the Background Papers, Canberra Report. The issue of leakage from civil stocks of plutonium is dealt with in "Control of Weapons-Usable Nuclear Materials," a paper delivered by George Bunn to the NPT Preparatory Committee, April 16, 1997. *The Economist*, in its lead editorial "Don't Ban the Bomb," January 4, 1997, provided a rationale for retention. The American arguments for continued nuclear deterrence are spelled out by Walter B. Slocombe, Under-Secretary of Defense for Policy, in testimony before the Senate Governmental Affairs Subcommittee on International Security, Proliferation, and Federal Services Hearing on Nuclear Weapons and Deterrence, February 12, 1997. The pressure inside the United States for change is reflected in "An American Legacy: Building a Nuclear-Weapon-Free World," a report of the Henry L. Stimson Center's Committee on Eliminating Weapons of Mass Destruction.

Chapter 9: Recognizing Moral Bankruptcy

The nature of a new global ethic is described in *A Global Ethic: The Declaration of the Parliament of the World's Religions*, New York: Continuum, 1995, which contains commentaries by Hans Kung and Karl-Josef Kuschel.

Chapter 10: Deciding to Hope

The Vaclav Havel quotation is from his book *The Art of the Impossible: Politics as Morality in Practice*, New York: Alfred A. Knopf, 1997. My views on hope owe much to the thinking of Dr. Ronna Jevne, Program Director of The Hope Foundation, Edmonton. Material from the ICIS Centre for A Science of Hope, 121 Avenue of the Americas, New York, N.Y. 10013, was also helpful.

Selected Web Sites

The Internet provides a wealth of current information on nuclear weapons and power issues around the world. Here is a listing of selected sites I use, most of which open into a vast range of linked sites. Also, *The Internet and the Bomb: A Research Guide to Policy and Information About Nuclear Weapons*, by William M. Arken and Robert S. Norris (Washington: Natural Resource Defense Council, 1997) lists hundreds of sites.

Abolition 2000

www.hookele.com/abolition2000/
A global network of more than 700 organizations that have endorsed the Abolition 2000 statement calling for states to negotiate by 2000 a Nuclear Weapons Convention to eliminate all nuclear weapons.

Canadian Coalition for Nuclear Responsibilities

www.ccnr.org
Dedicated to education and research on nuclear energy issues, civilian or military, and points to non-nuclear alternatives. Strong opponent of nuclear energy because fuels are too susceptible to theft by terrorists and the unsolved problem of radiation wastes. Monitors Candu reactors, opposes Atomic Energy of Canada and Ontario Hydro's plan to import 100 tons of weapons-grade plutonium over the next 25 years for Ontario Hydro's Bruce "A" nuclear reactors.

Canadian Disarmament Digest

www.dfait-maeci.gc.ca/english/foreignp/disarm/cddhome1.htm
A Canadian government site covering non-proliferation, arms control, and disarmament issues from a Canadian perspective. Seeks to encourage public discussion on these questions. Canadians are asked to comment on three questions concerning the World Court's Advisory Opinion on nuclear weapons.

Canadian Network to Abolish Nuclear Weapons

watserv1/.uwaterloo.ca/~plough/cnanw/cnanw.html
A network of Canadian peace groups working to build support for the goals of Abolition 2000 in Canada. Names, addresses of key contacts provided. Public discussions take place via e-mail. Write watserv1.vwaterloo.ca/-plough/cnanw/cnanw.html with only the message "subscribe abolition's e-Mail address" in the body of the text.

Canberra Commission on the Elimination of Nuclear Weapons

www.dfat.gov.au/dfat/cc/cchome.html
Full text of the Canberra Commission's report is available.

Center for Defense Information

www.cdi.org/main.html
An independent monitor of the U.S. military, CDI is a constant critic of excessive defence spending. Produces videos as well as publications.

Center for Non-Proliferation Studies at the Monterey Institute of International Studies

www.miis.edu/
Provides research tools, analysis, training on non-proliferation issues to scholars and policymakers from around the world. Works collaboratively with the Center for Contemporary International Problems, Moscow.

Global Anti-Nuclear Alliance

www.inter.nl.net/hcc/A.Malten/work.html
Provides information on actions, including civil resistance, to implement the World Court Advisory Opinion on nuclear weapons.

GlobeVote

www.sfu.ca/globevote/
This global network of universities and colleges, based at Simon Fraser University, Vancouver, B.C., has developed a report to the U.N. General Assembly to call the world's first global referendum

on nuclear disarmament. It's a fascinating site operating in Chinese, French, German, Italian, Portugese, Punjabi, Spanish, Czech, and English.

IALANA (International Association of Lawyers Against Nuclear Arms)

www.ddh.nl/org/ialana/index.html

Operating out of the Netherlands with affiliates around the world (including Canada) IALANA works to strengthen the international legal order to de-legitimize nuclear weapons. It is promoting the 1999 Hague Peace Conference, which will commemorate the 100th anniversary of the first Hague Peace Conference, a milestone in the development of international humanitarian law.

International Atomic Energy Agency

www.iaea.org/

World Atom, the IAEA's public information Internet service, provides a wide range of information on the international status of nuclear power and safeguards issues.

International Court of Justice (World Court)

www.un.org/Overview/Organs/icj.html

Summary of the World Court's Advisory Opinion on nuclear weapons along with summaries of separate opinions of judges is available on this site.

International Peace Bureau

www3.itu.int/ipb/

IPB is the world's oldest (founded in 1892) and most comprehensive international peace network, reaching into 40 countries. One of its priorities is women and peace. The site features "A Women's Peace Platform for the 21st Century," which begins with the visionary statement, "Women see a world without wars, weapons or violence. We see a society free of nuclear weapons, militarism and repression."

NATO

www.nato.int/welcome/home.htm

The home site of the Alliance of 16 Western nations — and soon to be more — deals with Alliance inter-action, European Security and Defence Identity, and the Partnership for Peace.

NGO Committee on Disarmament

www.igc.apc.org/disarm/
The NGO Committee, operating from the United Nations in New York, is an independent service organization for disarmament issues. It provides updates from the newspaper *Disarmament Times*, the "ABCs of Disarmament," and events and calendar information. It offers open channels for communication among citizens' groups, governments, and U.N. bodies.

Nuclear Control Institute

www.nci.org/nci/index.htm
Founded in 1981, the Washington-based research centre focuses on the urgency of eliminating plutonium and highly enriched uranium from civilian nuclear power and research facilities. It has a special section on the nuclear terrorism threat.

OSCE (Organization for Security and Cooperation in Europe)

www.osceprag.cz/
The OSCE, a pan-European security organization whose 55 participating states span the geographical area from Vancouver to Vladivostok, takes a comprehensive view of security, including human rights and development questions. Although overshadowed by NATO, the OSCE is taking a leading role in fostering security through cooperation in Europe.

PEACE wire

www.peacewire.org/
A cooperative effort between the Public Education for Peace Society, which provides resources to educators, and End the Arms Race, the coordinating peace organization for British Columbia. The site provides "Hot Topics," on-line resources, photo exhibits, and a Round-table Discussion Area.

Physicians for Global Survival

www.web.apc.org/~pgs/

A comprehensive site with many categories: arms, war, peace, health, human dignity, landmines. Its sections on the World Court Project and Abolition 2000 open into a wide range of information on the ramifications of the World Court's Advisory Opinion and the documents and activities of the citizens' movement to get negotiations for a Nuclear Weapons Convention completed by 2000. The related links are almost encyclopedic in content. Tolstoy, Schwartzer, Einstein-Russell Manifesto, Gorbachev, Rotblat — all the greats are here.

Project Ploughshares

watserv1.uwaterloo.ca/~plough/

Canada's ecumenical peace research organization based at Conrad Grebel College, Waterloo, Ontario. Specializes in Canadian themes and makes back issues of the quarterly *Monitor* available, including Bill Robinson's analysis, "Canada and Nuclear Weapons: Kicking the Nuclear Habit," June 1995. Provides: text of submissions to Parliamentary Committee reviewing Canada's nuclear weapons policies; annual Armed Conflicts Report; Canadian military exports by region, 1978-1995; recommendations for tightening Canada's military export control policies. Links to many church sites.

Pugwash Conference on Science and World Affairs

www.qmw.ac.uk/pugwash/home.html

The Nobel Peace Prize-winning organization brings together influential scholars and public figures concerned with reducing the danger of armed conflict. Has specialized in nuclear disarmament. Site offers major statements.

SIPRI (Stockholm International Peace Research Institute)

www.sipri.se/

The renowned SIPRI, in addition to its annual yearbook, publishes research on arms transfers, arms production, military expenditure, military technology, chemical and biological weapons, and European security.

The Henry L. Stimson Center

www.stimson.org
A non-profit, non-partisan research institute in Washington, D.C., concentrating on international security issues where policy, technology, and politics intersect. Contains American government documents and current speeches of international figures on global security issues.

The Year 2000 Campaign to Redirect World Military Spending to Human Development

www.fas.org/pub/gen/mswg/year2000/statemen.htm
Information on a campaign launched by Oscar Arias, Nobel Peace Laureate and former President of Costa Rica, to spend less on the military and more on human development.

United Nations

www.un.org/index.html
A wide-ranging view of the U.N., taking as main themes peace and security, economic and social development, international law, human rights, and humanitarian affairs. Many documents and current news releases are available.

United Nations Centre for Disarmament Affairs

www.un.org/depts/dpa/docs/cdahome.htm
Provides full information on global disarmament bodies and meetings, such as the First Committee, Disarmament Commission, and the Conference on Disarmament. The major international documents on disarmament are available.

Glossary

CTBT	Comprehensive Test Ban Treaty
IAEA	International Atomic Energy Agency
NATO	North Atlantic Treaty Organization
NGO	Non-Governmental Organization
NNWS	Non-Nuclear Weapons State(s)
NORAD	North American Aerospace Defence
NPT	Non-Proliferation Treaty
NWC	Nuclear Weapons Convention
NWS	Nuclear Weapons State(s)
START	Strategic Arms Reduction Talks
WHO	World Health Organization

Suggestions for Further Reading

Allison, Graham T., Owen R. Cote, Jr., Richard A. Falkenrath, and Steven E. Miller. *Avoiding Nuclear Anarchy: Containing the Threat of Loose Russian Nuclear Weapons and Fissile Material.* Cambridge, Mass.: MIT Press, 1996. As an open society, the United States has no reliable defence against smuggled weapons by a determined state or terrorist group. The only way to combat the threat is by preventing nuclear leakage in the first place.

Brown, Noel J. and Pierre Quiblier, eds. *Ethics & Agenda 21.* New York: United Nations, 1994. A number of essays spell out the moral grounding needed if the program of action laid out at the 1992 Earth Summit is to serve the interests of all humanity.

Clark, Roger S. and Madeleine Sann, eds. *The Case Against the Bomb.* Camden, N.J.: Rutgers University School of Law, 1996. Contains the text of the World Court Advisory Opinion on nuclear weapons, the testimony of the Marshall Islands, Samoa, and Solomon Islands, with an Introduction to the issues by Roger S. Clark.

Commission on Global Governance, report of, *Our Global Neighbourhood.* Oxford, U.K.: Oxford University Press, 1995. An international commission deals with human security at a time of immense change in the world and advocates global governance (not global government) based on the values of a global civic ethic.

Cortwright, David and Amitabh Mattoo, eds. *India and the Bomb: Public Opinion and Nuclear Options.* Notre Dame, Ind.: University of Notre Dame Press, 1996. India has been criticized for not signing the Comprehensive Test Ban Treaty. This book explains why nothing short of a time-bound program for global nuclear disarmament will sway India from keeping its nuclear options open.

Forsberg, Randell, William Driscoll, Gregory Webb, and Jonathan Dean. *Nonproliferation Primer: Preventing the Spread of Nu-*

clear, Chemical and Biological Weapons. Cambridge, Mass.: MIT Press, 1995. A useful resource book for beginners and experts alike, providing technical background needed to understand the full range of proliferation issues.

Havel, Vaclav *The Art of the Impossible: Politics as Morality in Practice.* New York: Alfred A. Knopf, 1997. Dissident and playwright Vaclav Havel, President of the Czech Republic, has collected a series of speeches asserting that common sense, moderation, responsibility, good taste, feeling, instinct, and conscience are the keys to long-term political success.

Kegley, Charles W. Jr., and Kenneth L. Schwab, eds. *After the Cold War: Questioning the Morality of Nuclear Deterrence.* Boulder, Colorado: Westview Press, 1991. The struggles ethicists are still having in deciding on the morality or immorality of nuclear weapons in the post-Cold War era are reflected in these informed essays.

Kung, Hans and Karl-Josef Kuschel, eds. *A Global Ethic: The Declaration of the Parliament of the World's Religions.* New York: Continuum, 1995. In 1993, the Parliament of the World's Religions took a historic step with its "Declaration Toward a Global Ethic." Representatives of the world's religions, great and small, signed a statement of a minimal ethic on which all could agree.

Lifton, Robert J. and Greg Mitchell. *Hiroshima in America: Fifty Years of Denial,* New York: G. P. Putnam's Sons, 1995. To mark the fiftieth anniversary of the atomic bombings of Hiroshima and Nagasaki, the authors assess the political, ethical and psychological impact of Hiroshima on the United States. Their thesis is that Americans are still unwilling to face the truth about Hiroshima.

Nardin, Terry, ed. *The Ethics of War and Peace: Religious and Secular Perspectives,* Princeton: Princeton University Press, 1996. The classic debate between natural law and political realism is dealt with in these recent essays, which try to expand the modern dialogue to include the views of Christianity, Judaism, and Islam

Powers, Gerard F., Drew Christiansen, and S.J., Robert T. Hennemeyer, eds. *Peacemaking: Moral and Policy Challenges for a New World,* Washington, D.C.: United States Catholic Conference, 1994. Convinced that religion and morality must be a prominent part of the debate about the shape of a new world order, this series of presentations deals with the challenges and opportunities involved in shaping a just and peaceful post-Cold War world.

Rotblat, Joseph, Jack Steinberger and Bhalchandra Udgaonkar, eds. *A Nuclear-Weapon-Free World: Desirable? Feasible?* Boulder, Colorado: Westview Press, 1993. A product of the Nobel Peace Prize-winning Pugwash movement, this book outlines why the elimination of nuclear weapons is no longer a fanciful idea but the focus of serious study.

Starke, Linda. *Signs of Hope: Working Towards Our Common Future*, Oxford: Oxford University Press, 1990. New initiatives on environmental protection taken by governments, industry, scientists, NGOs, and young people show the power of civil society — when it is moved to act.

Acknowledgments

The idea for this book emerged from a series of roundtable discussions of community leaders and activists in eighteen Canadian cities in September, 1996 that were originated by Project Ploughshares, a leading ecumenical organization dedicated to peace and social justice. Ernie and Nancy Reghr and Grant Birks provided support and encouraged me to proceed.

Research and publication were made possible by financial assistance from the Simons Foundation and the Anti-Nuclear-War Fund. I am particularly grateful to Dr. Jennifer Simons and Dr. Alan Phillips.

Judge Mohammed Bedjaoui, President of the International Court of Justice when it handed down its Advisory Opinion on nuclear weapons, honoured me by writing a Foreword. The phrase "the ultimate evil" was used by Judge Bedjaoui himself in describing nuclear weapons. I thank him for the leadership he has given this paramount issue.

Many helpful suggestions for improvement of the manuscript were made by three experts in nuclear disarmament who read a first draft: Tariq Rauf of the Monterey Institute of International Studies in Monterey, California; Bill Robinson, editor of the *Monitor*, a quarterly published by Project Ploughshares; and Alyn Ware, of the New York-based Lawyers' Committee on Nuclear Policy. Any remaining errors are mine alone.

I benefited from the views of many individuals, including Jonathon Granoff, Debbie Grisdale, Peter Weiss, Roger Clark, Ruth Bertelson, Bev Delong, James Turner Johnson, Robert Johanson, Gerard F. Powers, Rob Green, David Schwartz, and Ross Wilcock. They helped me in a variety of ways.

The University of Alberta's Political Science Department, chaired by Dr. Janine Brodie, continues to provide me with intellectual stimulus. The students in my seminar, "War or Peace in the Twenty-first Century," are a source of regeneration to me.

My editors at James Lorimer and Co. Ltd., Diane Young and Scott Milsom, gave me careful and considerate guidance in the development of this book. My research assistant, Jennifer Radford, found material when I needed it. My long-time assistant, Bonnie Payne, prepared the manuscript.

I owe a special debt of gratitude to Dr. Ronna Jevne, who taught me ways to find hope at a critical time in my life.

Douglas Roche
Edmonton, Alberta
July 23, 1997

Index

AGMV
MARQUIS
Québec, Canada
1997